13

An Immigration Tale

MOHI. B

AuthorHouse™ UK
1663 Liberty Drive
Bloomington, IN 47403 USA
www.authorhouse.co.uk
UK TFN: 0800 0148641 (Toll Free inside the UK)
UK Local: 02036 956322 (+44 20 3695 6322 from outside the UK)

Because of the dynamic nature of the Internet, any web addresses or links contained in
this book may have changed since publication and may no longer be valid. The views
expressed in this work are solely those of the author and do not necessarily reflect the views
of the publisher, and the publisher hereby disclaims any responsibility for them.

Any people depicted in stock imagery provided by Getty Images are models,
and such images are being used for illustrative purposes only.
Certain stock imagery © Getty Images.

This book is printed on acid-free paper.

ISBN: 978-1-7283-5421-7 (sc)
ISBN: 978-1-7283-5420-0 (e)

Print information available on the last page.

Published by AuthorHouse07/03/2020

authorHOUSE®

Acknowledgments

I didn't have words to say goodbye to the person who scolded me for not wearing a beanie and the person who framed my first drawing, and I still don't have words to show my gratitude. My mom and dad, I am no good with words when it comes to you, but thank you for being who you are. I really do mean it.

Alyaa and Rozaina, you weren't on this journey with us, but we shared the much more difficult journey called life, and you beat the hell out of it.

I would like to thank those who listened and chatted with me at midnight— my friends Hamza and Bedir—for always being there for me.

For those who preferred being in the rain and cold instead of pulling a blanket over their heads and sipping hot tea—the volunteers, the pure souls, the Red Cross, the UNHCR, and Team Humanity and Salam Aldeen—thank you.

I also want to take a moment to appreciate the support of my Instagram followers. That is correct: they are the main reason I took the risk and had the courage to take the first bold step towards writing my story. Thanking Instagram followers, huh? What a time to be alive.

Last but not least are the people whose names were mentioned countless times in the book, the ones who shared my journey. I would like to say thank you to Amer, who took the responsibility to guide us throughout the journey; to Haya, who did her best to fill my mother's shoes; to Mohamad, who always stayed back to help us and people who were in need; to Ghaithaa, who showed her kindness in the worst situations; to Othman, who never left my side the whole journey; to Abdo and Linda, who taught me patience; and to Ezz, without whose decision this book wouldn't exist.

And of course, thank you, the holder of this book, for picking it up and deciding to give it a try. Thank you for wanting to learn more about what we refugees have gone through.

Say, "Who delivers you from the darkness of land and sea?"

You call upon Him humbly and inwardly: "If He delivers us

from this, We will surely be among the thankful."

—Al-An'am, verse 63

1
When It All Began
"I am going to Germany."

I finally found a summer job after months of searching. I had recently graduated from high school, and it was time to work and save some money to pay for mathematics courses. I was good at math, but YÖS, the entrance examination for foreign students at Turkish universities, wasn't at all easy.

I worked in a small internet cafe that was a couple of blocks away from our apartment. During lunch, I would walk home and eat whatever delicious dish my mother made. Unfortunately, this routine lasted for only a month.

"Hey, Mohi, you don't need to come here tomorrow," said my boss at the cafe.

"Why? Is there something wrong?" I asked.

"No, but my cousin is looking for a job, and he wants to work here, so …"

My boss didn't bother to make up a white lie. Maybe it was better that he didn't. Anyway, this was the work life, as I knew it at least. With no other choices, I accepted my fate and was ready to search for other opportunities the next morning.

Before my last day ended, my cousin Ezz passed by to say hello. He did it every day, but it felt different this time.

"Did you finish your job early today?" I asked him.

"No," he said. "I took a leave."

"Why?"

"I want to go to Germany," he said firmly.

"Ezz, how many times do we need to go through th—"

"I know what you will say," he interrupted. "I just came to tell you that I am going."

"But … OK. We will talk when I get home."

It wasn't his first time talking about going to Germany. Whenever one of his friends left Turkey, Ezz would get hyped up. He kept in contact with them, and they encouraged him to leave Turkey for better opportunities in Europe. But at the end of the day, he always calmed down and went back to his work routine.

We'd had a huge influence on each other. His father died when he was a kid, and Ezz had been living with us since. He had always been a part of our family, and we never considered him a cousin but a brother.

My last working day was officially over. I walked home with my salary of 550 Turkish lira in my pocket—about 185 dollars. I was tired, not physically, but emotionally. To find this job in the internet cafe, I'd had to hear the phrase *Suriyeli yok*—"no Syrians"—hundreds of times. I wondered how many more times I was going to hear it before getting a new job.

I got home to find my aunt in the living room talking with my grandmother about someone's granddaughter's cousin who was getting married. My aunt lived on the same street and visited us twice or more a week. I didn't want to say that I lost my job in front of her, not even to my parents, because there was nothing they could do. It would only make them feel down.

My mother was in the kitchen reheating food from lunch to make dinner. Alyaa, my oldest sister, was preparing tea, while my father was figuring out a new method for engraving on stones. He had studied engineering in his youth, but his old age made finding a job in Turkey impossible, so he resorted to art.

The apartment was calm, as my brother's wife, Haya, was putting their 1-year-old twins to sleep. My brother Amer, her husband, was still at work. He worked late at night.

I went to my room—the small room I shared with Ezz and my brother Othman. It was furnished with two worn-out couches and an old thin mattress that I put between the couches to sleep on. Ezz was lying down and surfing social media, while Othman was studying mathematics and preparing for YÖS.

Othman is one year older than me and one year younger than Ezz. Everyone said that they were twins. In fact, they did look a lot alike. They were both tall, had similar facial expressions, and talked the same way. Ezz looked more like a brother to Othman than I did, but for me, I never understood why people mixed them up. Perhaps this was because I lived with them for almost eighteen years.

"Ezz, did you tell my parents about going to Germany?" I asked.

"No, I didn't."

"Then don't," I advised. "I understand that your job is exhausting and you have to work more than twelve hours a day, but going through the sea is just suicide."

"I told him, but he is dumb and won't listen," said Othman.

"Can we just not talk about it now?" Ezz ended the conversation, thankfully. I wasn't in a good mood either.

Later, we ate dinner all together—the typical and favourite dish, rice and chicken—before we all went to bed. The next day, I woke up before noon. I had to explain to my parents why I didn't have to wake up early. My aunt had left early and wasn't home. Ezz wasn't home either. I thought he must have gone to work and forgotten about yesterday's plans.

I was wearing my black pants and white sweater. I'd taken a shower using Othman's perfume—secretly, of course. It was time to search for a job. A CV wasn't needed. One just needed to go around in the street, walk into every store, and ask for a job.

Before I headed out, Ezz came home with a backpack and a lot of snacks. He sat in the living room, where everyone else was except Amer, who was at work.

"I am going to Germany," he announced.

"What are you saying, Ezz?" my mother gasped.

"I know you will try to convince me not to do it, as you did many times before, so I already bought the ticket from Istanbul to Izmir tomorrow. Izmir is a city near the Mediterranean Sea where people gather to take the boat to Greece."

"Ezz, listen to me," said my father sternly. "You cannot go. We have talked about this, and I won't let you do it."

"I know," Ezz replied, unmoved, "and I told you many times, I cannot waste my life here while all my friends are now in Germany and Sweden. I have worked twelve hours every day for a year, carrying goods from place to place, for only 700 Turkish lira, and for what? Nothing, for I am Syrian. I am still 20 years old, and I want to build my future. There is no future here for me!"

Silence took over for a moment. He had a point. Long working hours with a very low salary—no good future would come out of that.

"I also know that you are worried about me," continued Ezz, "but if you really wish me goodness and success, then you shouldn't stand in my way."

Once again, I agreed with his arguments. Still, I was against the idea of taking the rubber boat. But after what he said, I didn't feel like saying a word. No one did.

I put on my shoes and walked out and around, searching for a job. I skipped most of the stores without even asking if they offered a job. I didn't want to go back home, and I couldn't stop thinking of what Ezz had said. Was he serious this time? Would he do it for real? Couldn't he be more patient? It was going to be all right. It had to be all right.

While I was lost in the street and my thoughts, my phone rang. It was Ezz. He wanted to go say goodbye to my aunt and asked me to go with him.

It was evening when I went with Ezz and Othman to visit my aunt. Five minutes in, and Ezz got a phone call from my father.

"Leave everything and come home immediately," he said. "Your aunt and grandmother are crying."

My aunt heard what my father said and knew that Ezz had something to say. He explained everything to her. She wanted to believe that it was just one of those times when Ezz was talking about Germany, but he was serious this time. Then the crying started.

Ezz's phone rang again, but he declined the call and told my aunt that he had to see my mother and grandmother.

Before leaving, I reassured my aunt, "It is all right. He won't leave. He has done this many times before. I know him very well."

Yes, I knew him, and he still might change his mind. I wanted to believe that and only that.

When we arrived home, there was a distant relative with his wife and 6-year-old son who had just come from Sweden to visit Istanbul for two days.

My mother was broken. I could easily tell from her face. She had cried until her face turned red, yet she was trying her best to smile and look happy about meeting our guests.

We greeted the guest and sat with him. We naturally talked about and compared life in Turkey and Sweden.

"Turkey is a wonderful country, but it is hard to find a job," I said.

"Sweden is nice too," said our guest, "and you can take a course in cooking or driving to find a job easily."

I noticed that my father had been absent for a while. It was unusual that we had a guest in the living room and my father wasn't sitting with him. It wasn't considered a good gesture for welcoming a guest.

I went to see where my father might be and then met Haya coming out of our small room and closing the door carefully.

"What?" I asked.

"Hush!"

"What?" I asked again.

"You might go with Ezz tomorrow," Haya said.

"What?!"

"Quiet! I don't know. I just heard your father and Amer discussing it."

I went into the room with mixed emotions. I needed answers. My father was sitting on a couch, while Amer was sitting next to him talking on the phone. Before I opened my mouth, Ezz and Othman were standing behind me.

"What is going on?" asked Othman. "Is it true that we will go with Ezz tomorrow?"

"No. There is nothing for sure. We are just seeing if there is a possibility. Now go back and sit with the guest. It is impolite to leave him alone. And say nothing about this."

Our bodies were in the sitting room, but our minds were in the room with my father and Amer. Something big was being cooked up, and not even my mother knew about it. Meanwhile, we were drinking tea and eating cinnamon cookies that the guest had brought from Sweden.

A short while later, my father and Amer joined us and started welcoming and talking to the guest. Ezz gave me and Othman a look, and we left the living room.

"Amer, come, I need to ask you something," said Ezz. "I think my phone is broken."

"What is wrong with your phone?" asked Amer after he left the living room.

"Forget the damn phone," snapped Ezz. "Is it true? Are you coming with me?"

"I might be able to afford the money for me, Mohi, and Othman," said Amer.

"What about Mohammad?" I asked. "You know that he is suffering from his job and the rent."

"I will try to talk with the person who helped me with the money," said Amer, "but there is nothing for sure."

Instead of going back to the living room, we went to my brother Mohamad's apartment, which was on the same floor and opposite to ours.

"Hello! Come in!" His wife, Ghaithaa, opened the door.

Mohamad was sleeping on the couch. He was drained after working for over fifteen hours. He had to work many hours to pay the rent—not that he liked it. He talked with his boss about increasing his salary, but his boss said that if he talked about salary again, he could go and find another job.

"We are going with Ezz tomorrow," I told Ghaithaa. She giggled and asked whether we wanted coffee or tea.

"He is not kidding," Othman chimed in. "We might actually follow Ezz tomorrow."

We woke Mohamad up and told him what my father and Amer were planning. He thought we were joking and covered his head to go back to sleep, until we swore that we were not.

After we told them what was happening, we needed to go back and get more information. We returned home with butterflies in our stomachs. The guest was still there. Only half an hour had passed since he came, and half an hour wasn't enough time for someone who came all the way from Sweden to visit my family. We knew we had to suffer for a lot longer and not talk about our future that might be changing forever.

Two hours later, the guest decided to leave. He shook hands with every one of us, put on his shoes slowly, had a ten-minute conversation at the door, and then finally left with his family.

Then the room exploded with questions.

"What?!"

"Really?!"

"How?!"

"When?!"

"Impossible!"

Amer wasn't satisfied with his condition in Turkey. Although he and Mohamad had more than five years of experience in data and computers, they couldn't find a job in their specialty. Amer worked in a warehouse, and his salary was just enough to help to pay the rent and buy milk and diapers for his toddlers. It was so stressful that he turned partly bald.

When he heard that Ezz had decided to go to Germany, he started considering it for real as well. He talked to his friend on the phone who agreed to lend him some money in addition to what Amer could save from his job.

Before my father and Amer started contacting friends and acquaintances in Germany, Sweden, and Norway, asking them about the living conditions and comparing them with each other, Mohamad and Ghaithaa joined us.

We still weren't taking it seriously, but we were rather excited about us going with Ezz.

"Listen, go to Sweden! The nature of the Scandinavian countries is breathtaking," said Alyaa.

"We are not looking for the beauty of nature," said Amer. "We need to see which country has the best future. I think Germany has more job opportunities."

"Not only job opportunities. Studying in Sweden is much better than Germany, as the guest said," added Othman.

"Calm down, people," I said. "I know how we can decide."

I tore a piece of paper into three and wrote on them *Germany*, *Sweden*, and *Norway*. I also added another piece of paper and wrote *USA* on it.

When we'd first come to Turkey, we'd applied for a resettlement program with the United Nations High Commissioner for Refugees (UNHCR) and got accepted to the USA. Unfortunately, our file had stayed suspended for one and a half years without any updates, and we'd lost hope.

"OK," I said. "I will shuffle these papers, and we will have to go to whatever we pick."

I let my grandmother draw first. She picked a paper, and it was Sweden. I let both Abdo and Linda, the boy and girl twins of Amer and Haya, pick a paper. Surprisingly, Sweden was picked three times!

"So, Sweden it is!" I said for fun.

It was starting to get real, and we had to decide which country was the best option for us before Ezz left so that we could stay together. After a lot

Ezz taking a photo of himself, Mohamad, Othman, me, and my father

of comparing and studying the whole situation in detail, we decided that our country of destination would be Sweden.

It was already past bedtime. We hadn't bought the tickets yet. We hadn't decided if we were even going. It was all planning, and we knew for sure that tomorrow would be a busy day.

After we all went to our rooms, the excitement turned into worrying, the joking turned into reality, and the tension began to permeate my mind. I couldn't stop thinking about the next day.

Are we going to Sweden? I wondered. *Are we taking the rubber boat and risking our lives in the sea where thousands of people have died? Why are we even going to Sweden? My brothers are free to go, but I don't really want to go. I want to stay with my parents. I am the youngest. I will wake up early tomorrow and find a job no matter what. I am staying here.*

Although we were nine persons and two toddlers living in a three-room apartment, throughout our residence in Turkey, my parents had welcomed many people—relatives, distant relatives, families, individuals, and even people we'd never met—to stay in our place for weeks and months preparing for their journey to Europe. I was totally against the idea of throwing myself in a rubber boat in the middle of the sea. I used to hear them saying that it wasn't that bad and many survived, but I wouldn't tell them not to go. They'd already made their decision and wanted to believe and feel safe that it was going to be all right.

But was it our turn now? Was it our time to take that road?

More and more thoughts rained down on me. I needed someone to talk to, even though my parents had insisted we shouldn't mention anything to anyone. I picked up the phone. It was late, and I didn't expect my friends to answer, but they did.

First, I texted my friend Hamza that I was leaving Turkey tomorrow and taking the rubber boat. I felt his shock and protest, especially since we had talked about the whole rubber-boat thing and that we were against it. He pretended to support my decision and told me that it was better for my sake. He also sent me some cat photos to ease me, as he knew I adored them.

My other friend, Bedir, couldn't hide his feelings.

"OK, but aren't you at least going to say goodbye face to face?" he asked.

"No," I replied.

"Not even to me?"

"Especially you."

I hate moments of farewell, especially unplanned ones. I used to see Bedir nearly every day, but it seemed like that wouldn't be the case anymore. I'd picked up the phone thinking that it would make me feel better, but I ended up with nothing but depression and sadness.

In the middle of my misery, the idea that I was going to leave my parents, the reason I was alive, hit me hard. I washed my face immediately in cold water to push it away and forced myself to sleep at four in the morning.

2
An Unplanned Farewell
"I don't want to go. Please tell him to go away. Mama, do something!"

The following day, everybody was up earlier than the birds. The dreaded day had come. Ezz was supposed to leave at noon, and Amer was looking for tickets to buy. He found available tickets at 20:30, which was too late.

There was no refund if Ezz had to cancel his ticket, and it would only add extra cost, so we agreed to meet him in Izmir. Unwillingly, I went with Othman to the supermarket to buy some snacks for us and Amer. We bought chocolates, cakes, and dates—things that wouldn't get ruined fast and made us feel full.

Amer wasn't home when we arrived. Haya dolefully said that he'd gone out to buy us life jackets. I couldn't believe that we were doing this. But we were, and Amer was buying life jackets. I had never imagined that I would get such negative feelings out of life jackets.

Ezz said that he would buy one in Izmir. He was preparing his backpack to only contain some clothes and snacks. It felt like he was going for a picnic, but he was about to travel to a whole new world.

It was time for him to leave. He hadn't told his mother in Egypt yet, so he called her.

"Ezz," she said, "you sound different. Is there something you want to say? Are you hiding something?"

"No ... actually yes," he admitted. "I am going to Germany."

"What?!" she exclaimed. "Are you crazy?! Are you messing with me?!"

"I bought the ticket, and I am leaving in half an hour."

"But why? Give me your aunt," she insisted.

"Mom, please don't make it more difficult," begged Ezz. "It is going to be all right."

"Oh Ezz ... my little angel, please don't die. Don't drown before I see you again. Please take care of yourself, my angel!"

As his mother sobbed, Ezz's face grew red. He didn't say a word. He wanted to cry and shout, but he just closed his eyes and listened to his mother break his heart until Alyaa took the phone from him and talked to his mother to calm her down.

Ezz stayed still on his knees in the middle of the living room before my mother hugged him. He threw himself in her lap and cried so heavily and loudly that he ran out of breath. Then there was our grandmother, who loved Ezz more than anyone in her life. Everybody in the family knew that Ezz was her precious boy.

He picked himself up, lifted his backpack onto his shoulders, and met my father's eyes.

"Darn you, boy. Do you really have to leave us?" asked my father, shedding a tear. It was the first time I saw him crying.

Before getting out, Ezz hugged me and Othman and told us that he would be waiting for us. Thank God it was a temporary farewell. I never knew how I would say goodbye to Ezz. My mind couldn't even make up a scenario for that.

He kissed my father, mother, and grandmother on the forehead, waved goodbye to Alyaa and Haya, and left the apartment. My grandmother, for whom walking was difficult, rushed to the balcony with my mother to watch Ezz leaving them for the last time. My parents had just said goodbye to their first son.

Before we had a chance to pull ourselves together, Amer called my father.

"I found a cheaper smuggler for 1,000 dollars a person. We don't have to pay for the toddlers. Ezz paid 1,200 dollars. We will take the rubber boat from a village in the west. I know we won't meet Ezz before leaving, but we still can meet him in Greece. This way, we can save some money for Mohamad to go with us. Tell Mohamad to prepare himself. We should be leaving at 19:00."

The plan had changed, but for the better. Mohamad was leaving my parents as well now. I was happy for him. He lived on only 25 dollars a month, and he'd always wanted to leave Turkey, but he never talked about it, as he knew he could never afford to go to Europe. I felt sorry, though, that my parents were going to lose another child.

I knocked on his door, and Ghaithaa opened it.

"Tell Mohamad to prepare himself," I told her. "He is leaving with us."

She didn't giggle this time. She read my face and cried. Mohamad came when he heard her crying, and she cried even more. They had been married for only two months. She was alone in Turkey. She had only Mohamad, and now they were about to live separately.

My aunt had no clue that we were leaving. She was probably still crying about Ezz, so I went with Othman to deliver more bad news to her. She opened the door, and her welcome wasn't so warm. I couldn't blame her.

She wanted to make us some tea, but we told her that we were in a hurry.

"What are you saying?" she asked.

"Yes, I know. It wasn't planned. It all happened yesterday," I told her. "We are sorry."

"But you always wanted your aunt to come to Turkey, and when she did, you are leaving her alone," she complained. "The ones I used to argue with are leaving. With whom am I going to argue now?"

No words came out of my mouth. We used to argue and fight a lot, and that was what made our relationship unique. She scolded us as kids, and when we grew up, we left her heartbroken. I always knew that her heart wasn't made of stone, but I didn't expect it to be so soft.

As much as I wanted to stay longer at her place, I had the person I adore the most in my mind: my mother. I wanted to spend every remaining second with her. I wanted to hug her for hours.

The way back home felt so far. I kept walking and walking but still couldn't reach home. I started jogging and ended up running as fast as I could racing with Othman. I saw my mother sitting on a chair on the balcony with her head bent to the wall.

I could see her pale face and red eyes from afar. I ran up the stairs and forced myself to take a deep breath. My father opened the door, and Othman jumped at him, crying.

I walked slowly to the balcony, wearing a fake smile on my face, pretending to be fine. I wanted to act like an adult, to show her that there was nothing to worry about, but the moment I saw her lifeless face, I became a 4-year-old child sobbing in his mother's lap and not wanting to let go. I sobbed into her chest unceasingly, hands clutching at her waist. She held me in silence, rocking me slowly as my tears soaked her clothes.

I was facing the very thing I had tried to ignore and push away. I was on my knees screaming silently and inhaling heavily. I felt nothing but pure sorrow. Every other emotion was pushed from my being.

"Mama, please forgive me … I am sorry for everything I have done. Please, I love you, please, I don't want to leave you … I swear to God that I'll come back to you, even if I have to crawl the way back …"

"Take good care of yourself and your brothers," she croaked while patting my head. "Don't argue with Othman, and stay together with Ezz when you meet him. Don't forget to wear your scarf and beanie and change your wet clothes immediately after you get out of the sea so you don't get sick."

Mother, what is in your head? Are you still thinking of me in such moments? Are you still worried about me getting cold? Don't you think about yourself for a moment? Don't you have a little mercy on your soul? Please, forget everything and just hug me.

They say that a mother's emotion overwhelms her logic; little do they know. My mother put her emotion away and gave me a lesson about the weather and clothes.

When I was depressed, she was the only one who could show me the way. When I felt not worthy, she made me feel like a king. When I felt like I wasn't loved, she gave me all the love in the world. How great can a mother be?

"Did you pray?" she asked.

"No," I admitted.

"Me neither. Let's pray together."

I held her hand as we went to her room. In my prayers, I said, "God, you have always been merciful with me, but this time I am in so much pain. I need you, once again, to be by my side. And please make it easier for my parents."

Later, at 15:00, Amer rang my father again to say, "I am sorry, Dad, I won't be able to say goodbye face to face. We will leave earlier. A driver is coming to pick my brothers up at 17:00."

Wait! That is in two hours!

My heart started beating faster. I wasn't yet prepared to say goodbye to my parents. I would never be prepared to do so. I was about to have a mental breakdown when my father interrupted my and everybody else's thoughts by saying, "Haya, do you want to go with your husband?"

"What about the children?" she replied after a long pause.

"It is for the babies' sake," my father said. "By the time Amer arrives in Sweden, the family reunification laws might change, and you and the toddlers might be separated from their father for years."

"But there isn't enough money," she pointed out.

"I talked with my brother in China, and he sent me some money," my father replied. "Amer can pick it up today."

I was stunned. Did my father just agree to let his 1-year-old grandchildren take the rubber boat? Before moving to Turkey, he had spent days and nights studying the situation and checking the prices, job opportunities, high schools and even weather, and now, in minutes, he had decided to risk the lives of two innocent toddlers.

Haya opened the closet hesitantly and started packing some clothes and diapers for the children.

"Mohi, tell Ghaithaa to prepare herself too," said my father.

He wasn't joking, and I wasn't surprised. At that moment, if someone had told me elephants could fly, I would believe him.

"Come on, you guys, what is going on? Why is everybody leaving all of a sudden?" protested Alyaa.

"The same thing applies to Ghaithaa. She might not see Mohamad in years, so she better go with him as well," said my father.

I knocked on the apartment door. Ghaithaa opened it, and I saw that she had been crying because Mohamad was leaving.

"Prepare yourself," I said. "We are leaving together in an hour."

Then she started bawling that *she* was leaving.

"Really? Ghaithaa can come with me?" asked Mohamad. "But we don't have money for her."

"Yes, I think it is better if she does," said our father. "I have half the amount for her. But you should talk with the smuggler to lower the price for you a bit."

"I can try," said Mohamad. "First, I am going to talk to my boss about giving me some money."

"Don't," our father advised him. "If he knows you are leaving, he won't give you any money."

"I know; he is very stingy. That is why I will tell him that I need to take my wife to the hospital urgently and ask for the salary of the days I worked this month."

Alyaa made a video call to my sister Rozaina in Egypt. I forgot I had a lovely sister in Egypt, but saying goodbye to her over the phone was the last thing I wanted to do. She burst into tears and then went crazy, to the point where we felt we were definitely going to drown. Her husband had to end the video call to calm her down.

Then Othman lost control. He started throwing his clothes out of his backpack and yelled that he didn't want to leave.

"No, you go," I said. "I will stay here with our parents. I am the youngest, and I still have a lot in my life to do. You should be studying at university already, but you couldn't. You should take the chance."

My parents didn't force us to leave, but they also knew it was for the best. My father discussed the situation with us again and reminded us how hard we had been trying to study at universities but couldn't because of the high costs. He didn't want us to end up like Mohamad and Amer. They both had certificates and experience, and it was pretty challenging for them to work in high-position jobs as Syrians.

"I don't understand why you are making a scene," he said. "After about one year in Sweden, you will get your permit, and then you will be able to visit us as many times as you wish. You will have more chances in Sweden than in Turkey. You will be able to attend university and get a good job. If you stay in Turkey you won't make any progress. You will waste your life in work only."

His lecture was shorter this time. We only had a few minutes before leaving. He pacified us and put the clothes back in the backpack.

Amer rang again and told us that the driver would arrive in ten minutes.

Mohamad came back with the money. He and Ghaithaa were ready. Haya was prepared. Alyaa was hugging both Abdo and Linda and crying.

In ten minutes, my life would change. Our lives would change. What should I do? Where should I go? There was nothing to do except throw myself in my mother's lap. Like ten minutes was enough time to say goodbye to my parents. Like my lifetime was enough.

Beep beep.

"No!" I screamed at the sound of the horn. "No! No! I don't want to go. Please tell him to go away. Mama, do something!"

She hugged me and Othman harder. The thousand oceans of tears she had been holding back streamed down her face. Othman was screaming too, but I could hear no one. I was just denying the reality around me.

Ghaithaa came closer and tried to speak to me, but I pushed her away. Although it was hard for everybody, they just stayed and watched us grieving and suffering.

The driver had been waiting for five minutes. I didn't care. Still, sooner or later, we had to go.

I lifted my head up, feeling dizzy. My eyes were full of tears, and my vision was blurred. Suddenly, I felt so warm. My father hugged me. The man who hardly ever hugged me, the man who was rarely seen at home, the man who bought me a house at the age of 13, the man who framed my first drawing, the man who was my friend, was crying.

He said nothing. He didn't need to. He always let his actions speak about him. My grandmother was on her feet kissing my face and saying endless prayers. Her voice was so weak that I understood nothing. She almost fainted, and I had to make her sit down again.

We reached the door, and I saw Alyaa standing alone and sobbing. She indeed had the warmest heart in the whole world. She was the oldest, and I was the youngest. She was like a mother to me.

"Don't forget your God there," she said. "God is not only in Turkey. He is everywhere. Take good care of your brothers. We are waiting for you." She was just as strong as my mother.

My mom wanted to take photos of us. I snatched her phone and threw it away and told her that these photos would only become bad memories to break her heart. I hugged my parents once again and went down to the van.

Our crying noises brought up the neighbours and the people on the street. They were looking at us curiously. We couldn't care less.

We put our baggage in the van, and before getting in, I saw Alyaa and my grandmother on the balcony, and my mother running down the stairs with my father shouting our names. I ran back and kissed their foreheads.

Destiny isn't always gentle. It let me escape the farewell with my friends and Ezz, but it didn't let me escape saying goodbye to my parents.

We got in the van. It drove away. My sight was only on my parents. My mother covering her mouth and my father holding her close to him was the last thing I saw.

3
Humiliation
"Go back to your seat, you bloody boy!"

Saturday/10-10-2015/17:25

No one was talking in the van. Everyone was quiet. The only thing we heard was the Quran playing on the radio. The driver kept looking at us through the rear-view mirror. He was desperate to say anything that would make us feel better, but he knew that there was nothing and decided to stay silent.

Mohamad was recording a video from the front seat. Ghaithaa sat in front of Othman with Linda on her lap, and Haya sat next to me carrying Abdo, who was asleep.

I laid my head on the window watching the road I used to take to school every day for the last time. I was still thinking of what had happened half an hour ago. My mind kept repeating all the scenes as if on a screen in invisible space.

Will I see them again? Or is it all over? Did that happen in only one day?

After half an hour of outer silence and inner chaos, we arrived at Fatih, where Amer waited for us with a huge black plastic bag filled with life jackets.

"I hope you will reach Greece safely," said the driver after we got off. Then he drove away to get more people like us, to drive them to their new life.

"There is a park near here that we need to walk to and wait for a call from the smuggler," said Amer. "I talked to him about Ghaithaa, and he agreed that we pay 800 USD for her. I also picked up the money that your uncle sent from China."

I didn't know if he was lucky for not having to say goodbye face to face or not. But he was as depressed as us.

As we reached the park, we saw many Syrian families already there. It didn't take us a long time to understand that they were also waiting for a call from the smuggler. We put our stuff on the only empty picnic table and waited for the call.

Half an hour passed. It became dark, but there were still no updates.

"Othman, Mohi, here, go buy some food." Amer handed us some money.

We hadn't had anything since the evening before. We had forgotten we were hungry. There were many more important things to take care of than food. We bought shawarma rolls to feed our starving bodies.

After we finished eating, we wrote down our phone numbers plus the Greek coastguard number in case we got separated, lost, or drowned.

"Damn. He is not answering," said Amer. "Ezz's phone is out of coverage. I didn't want to mention this to your parents, but I heard that the police are preventing people from taking the rubber boat from Izmir and arresting them."

"Maybe he already took the boat," said Mohamad.

I really hoped he had.

The cold weather didn't cool my feelings down. I felt alone despite being surrounded by many people: a father looking at his family, knowing that he might lose versus the sea and not be able to rescue them; a child asking his mother why she was crying; the mother lying to him and telling him that something got into her eye; a young guy holding his wife's hand and telling her that nothing bad was going to happen, although deep down he knew they were going to face the worst and might not make it out alive. All of them had their own story, just like us. Maybe worse.

Many cars were driving by, and many people were walking by. Some were busy, talking on their phones, and others were hanging out with friends. They had no clue why so many people were gathering in the park. They didn't know our stories.

All I wanted to do was grab someone by the arm and whisper—or maybe yell—that I was going to take the rubber boat, that I was leaving my family and going into the unknown.

I hate to admit it, but life stops for no one. I looked at the Historia Mall in front of me. Weeks ago, I had planned a surprise birthday party with my friends, and we laughed so hard that I could still hear the laughter in my head.

How would my friends react when they found out I left without telling them? Would they be mad at me or would they understand? Would they miss me if I drowned? At least Bedir and Hamza could tell them.

The metro station was only a three-minute walk. I knew how to go home. I could go home with my eyes closed. I had 15 lira in my transit card—more than enough to reach home. My parents were only an hour away. I could end all of this.

A guy parking his old motorbike caught my attention. With a cigarette in his mouth, he grabbed a big speaker and connected it to his phone. I wasn't the only one watching him curiously; almost everybody did. Minutes later, when he was all set, all the hidden emotions showed up as tears. He chose the worst time and place to play a sad song out loud in the public about people who drowned in the sea. Maybe he wanted to comfort us, but all we got was pessimism. He repeated it twice before he finally got on his motorcycle and rode away.

It was 21:00. No call yet.

The long wait made me consider going back for real. I'd already thought of a plan. I would tell my brothers that I needed to go to the bathroom and take the metro home instead. *Move. Move!* I told myself repeatedly. But my legs refused to move. I was in an unpleasant dream, a nightmare, watching myself screaming for help and not being able to control my body.

Before I could take a step, Amer got a call. "Hi," a voice said. "The buses have arrived and are waiting in the square near the park. Go there immediately."

It was too late to escape. My life was about to change forever.

Within seconds, the news spread amongst the people. We all picked up our bags and started moving. When we arrived at the square, two buses were waiting there. People rushed to the buses. We and other families had strollers, and we were struggling to fit them into the crowded baggage compartment.

The driver's assistant jumped off the bus, threw the strollers away, and shouted at us to get on the bus instantly. In two minutes, everyone got on the buses, and we were moving.

The bus was old with shabby seats. The lights inside the bus were off—obviously, because we were illegal. We were the last to get on, so we sat in the front seats. I sat with Othman, Mohamad sat with Ghaithaa, and Amer sat with Haya holding the toddlers. The bus was almost full of women, old people, and kids.

Ten minutes later, a loud police car siren was heard. It was after us, and the police pulled our bus over. The bus stopped on the highway, and both the driver and his assistant got off to talk with the police officers. How did the police know about the bus? Were they tracking us?

Many questions in my head needed answers. We couldn't hear what the tall and skinny driver and the short and fat assistant were saying to the police, but once we saw the driver putting money into the officer's hand, it was all clear. It was an obvious bribe, and the thrill of us being caught and sent back home vanished.

After half an hour, our bus stopped in a rest area near the highway. Without saying a word, the driver and his assistant turned off the engine and the air conditioning and walked away. We didn't know why they left. We waited for fifteen minutes, but nobody showed up.

The bus had fixed windows. We tried to open the door, but it was locked. Mohamad told Amer to call the smuggler and tell him what was going on.

"Where did the driver go, man?" Amer asked the smuggler. "We have been on the bus for fifteen minutes with closed windows and a locked door. We can barely breathe. Call the driver and tell him to come back and open the door!"

We waited for ten more minutes, but they didn't come back. Amer tried to call the smuggler again, but he didn't answer. There could be only one explanation. We'd been kidnapped!

There was no oxygen left to breathe, and it became extremely warm on the bus. People were coughing, and children were crying. We had to act.

Amer and Mohamad tried to break open the door and crush the front window. Othman and I turned on the SOS flashlight on our phones to draw someone's attention. We succeeded. A truck was parking around twenty metres away. The driver got out and walked slowly towards us. He looked careful and concerned, but when he got closer, he could see that there were people waving for help. He rushed to the bus and tried to open the door from the outside. He couldn't.

He pulled out his phone and typed in some numbers just as the driver and the assistant came running up and yelling at him to stop. They said that he didn't have to worry and that they'd had to leave for five minutes to use the washroom. The truck driver walked back to his truck in doubt, but he didn't want to get himself into trouble.

"What the hell are you doing?" barked the assistant in Turkish. "Do you want the police to know about us?"

Before hearing our complaints, they got out and were about to lock the door again when Amer threatened them. "If you lock the door again, I will call the police myself!"

The assistant didn't like the way Amer talked to him, but Amer sounded serious, so they left the door open.

Shortly after they left, they came back with a large group of people who seemed to be from Afghanistan. There were enough empty seats for around seven people on the bus, but according to the driver's logic, those seven empty seats could fit a group of people. The bus was so full that many people had to sit or lie down on the bus floor.

Four hours of driving passed. We were away from the cities, and the other bus that had arrived with ours in Fatih was driving ahead of us. Suddenly, the bus broke down on a mountain road. The driver made several attempts to start the bus engine, but it wouldn't start. He got off along with his assistant to check on the problem and ask for help from the driver and the assistant of the other bus.

We were stuck in the middle of nowhere for half an hour surrounded by nothing but darkness until the engine started again. This time, the driver didn't turn on the air conditioner. Eventually, it became uncomfortable on the bus. I went to ask the driver to turn the air conditioner on. It wasn't like I was asking for a life of luxury; we were having a bad time breathing.

"Excuse me," I said, "can you please turn on the air conditioner?"

"What the hell did you say?" the assistant replied.

"The air conditioner. Can you turn it on? It is really hot, and the children are crying"

"*Can you turn it on*," he mimicked me as he copied my voice. "Go back to your seat, you bloody boy!"

Insolence was the first impression he gave us, but I was shocked by the way he talked to me. I stood there for a moment considering my options—to start a fight or go back to my seat. I chose the second option and sat back in my seat feeling insulted and irritated. I didn't know if it was the right option, but I didn't like what had happened, nor did my brothers.

The temperature kept on increasing, and the heat quickly became unbearable.

"Turn on the air conditioner," said Amer.

"The air conditioner will not be turned on!" the assistant called out without looking back at Amer.

"I said, turn on the air conditioner!" Amer was losing his temper.

"Sit down right now!"

"The air conditioner will be turned on whether you like it or not!" said Mohamad, joining the argument.

After a lot of yelling and swearing, Amer said threateningly, "My phone is in my hand. One click, and the police will hear what I say. I don't care if you and I get thrown in jail. The only thing I care about is that you will turn on the goddamn air conditioner. So, for the last time, turn it on, or I swear, I will ring the police!"

The driver, who had been silent all this time, grabbed his assistant's hand and commanded him to sit down. They both mumbled something for a bit before turning the air conditioner on without further argument. We won a battle that should never have existed in the first place.

The bus broke down several more times. It was old, and the driver was terrible. Driving with him was like being on a roller coaster rather than a bus.

A couple of hours later, our bus and the bus in front of us stopped. It wasn't because of the engine this time. There were two buses and two all-black cars waiting for us. The driver and his assistant didn't freak out and it seemed that they were planning to meet with these cars. The driver got a call, apparently from one of the black cars, before continuing.

Everyone was quiet. Everything was quiet. There was only the noise of the bus wheels crushing gravel and stones. Then, without a warning, a bright flashlight shined in our eyes, causing us to lose our sight for some seconds. While covering my eyes with my arm, I looked through the window to see several police cars hiding behind the rocks. It was an ambush!

The police officers pointed their guns at us. I could feel the driver's and the assistant's fear and panic as they whispered and swore. The assistant got off the bus wearing a fake smile and said in a friendly tone I'd have never expected he could muster, "*Assalamu alaikum*—peace be upon you, brother."

"May you never find peace. Go back to where you came from, you goddamn shit!" fumed the police officer.

With no further argument, the assistant got back on the bus. Despite the tension and stress I felt, I was thrilled to see him treated like he should be. We thought that it was over. The police would arrest us and send us back to Istanbul. Unexpectedly, however, they just forced us to drive away.

4
A Million Stars
"I wished nothing but death."

Sunday/11-10-2015/00:37

We sat on the ground, drank some water, and washed our faces after we drove to a gas station on a highway where two other buses were waiting as well. It had been eleven hours straight since we got on the bus. Our bodies had become one with the seats.

At dawn, the two completely dark cars showed up. Men wearing all black and carrying guns on their waists came out. They had a little meeting with the drivers of the four buses and gave them the new instructions.

We were told to get back on the bus. All the buses followed the two black cars. We had to take a different road that the police didn't know about yet. It was time for plan B.

We reached a small village where the two cars left us, and the buses drove onto a ferry that drove us to an island. After four more hours of driving, we were finally on top of a mountain that overlooked the sea. I was glad to step out of the bus forever, glad that I would never see the face of the devil again. It was the first farewell that I liked.

Two guys wearing casual clothes and pistols on their waists were waiting for us. They were also smugglers.

"OK, everybody, we are going down. Follow us!" they said after we retrieved our bags.

We followed their steps down the rocky path. Guys were moving more smoothly than families, so one of the smugglers had to slow down and guide us. It took us forty-five minutes to catch up with the guys who waited for us on a sandy craggy piece of ground with some curvy trees fifteen metres above the sea.

Something didn't feel right. I was aware that the guys got down faster, but there were more Syrian and Afghani guys and families already there than those we came with. Like everyone else, we started putting on our life jackets and preparing for the rubber boat, but a smuggler told us that we had to wait a bit.

The other smuggler picked up some guys to help him carry some stuff, which we found out later was the rubber boats and their engines.

"Everyone get down! Don't make a noise!" shouted the smugglers all of a sudden.

The Turkish coastguard was patrolling around the island in search of smugglers. The smugglers got up and paced around while talking on their phones. We waited impatiently for them to finish talking and asked them again when we were supposed to leave.

Their answer was, "Not so soon."

We were on an island but not on a vacation, and the weather wasn't sunny. A rough woollen blanket of grey angry clouds took over the blue sky, and we knew that we were to be caught in a downpour, so we had to seek shelter like the others. We found a place between two big old trees.

It was raining heavily, and the dirt was turning quickly into mud. We took out our clothes from the bags and arranged them on top of the branches to keep the rain from creating a swamp. We weren't proud of our little shelter project, as the family next to us sat in a tent. We hadn't thought of that.

Amer tried to call Ezz and the smuggler in Istanbul, but the signal was poor. The life jackets were bothering us, so we took them off and waited for the sky to be gentle with us. Hours later, after everyone got soaked, the rain stopped.

The Turkish island

The man of the family who sat in the tent approached us and said, "Hello there! Dear God, you are all so wet!" He had a thick beard and smiling eyes.

"Unfortunately, we weren't as bright as you to get a tent," replied Amer.

"Ha ha, I have learned my lesson. I have been here since yesterday," he explained.

That made sense. We came along with three other buses, but there were way more people on the island. People had already been here before we arrived. But it also meant that we might spend the night on the island.

"This is my fifth time trying to go to Europe, but I have bad luck," the man said. "Every time, we get caught by the police, and they send us back to the province we came from. I hope we can make it this time."

"Are you serious? You mean there is still a chance we'll get caught and sent back?" sputtered Mohamad.

"Yes, but since this island is a new point, I am hoping that we can make it. Last time, I and my family tried to enter Europe by truck. We were around fifty people in cattle truck." He noticed our shock and continued. "We were told that there would be only twenty people in an empty truck. We were deceived. Of course, I protested and wanted to go back, but they forced us to get on the truck and threatened us with their weapons."

"For real?" Amer interrupted him.

"Wait, it gets worse," the man went on. "The truck driver left us in the dead of night in the middle of nowhere and ran away. We had to call the police to rescue us. Thank God we made it out alive. Not everyone did. There was a man with his 9-year-old boy in the truck. We ran out of oxygen, and the little boy suffocated to death in his father's lap. The father literally lost his mind."

Although we had heard such tragic stories on the news, hearing the story from someone who survived it left us speechless. We considered going back to Istanbul. We weren't the only ones.

"When are we moving?" A man with grey hair was arguing with the smuggler.

"You need to wait. The sea is rough, and the weather is unsteady."

"Well, it wasn't like this when we first came here, and you also

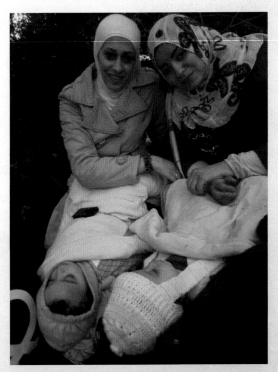

Ghaithaa and Haya putting
Abdo and Linda to sleep

told us to wait. Anyway, I am no longer staying here. I am going back with my family."

"You will not go back." The smuggler growled as he pointed his pistol at the man. "If you get caught by the police, everyone will be in trouble. You understand?"

The man wanted to argue further, but he hesitated and then nodded in silence. The smuggler walked away, leaving us shocked. But we weren't expecting good treatment from him.

Sometime later, when the smuggler wasn't around, the man took the chance and walked away with his wife and two children. People tried to convince him to stay and not get them into trouble, but he was determined.

Amer kept on trying to reach the smuggler in Istanbul until he finally could make a call. He mentioned that the smuggler hadn't mentioned staying for eight hours in the rain.

"I understand," said the smuggler, "but as you can see, taking the sea now is deadly. You better wait."

Although we weren't supposed to spend the day on the island, the smuggler was right. The sea was dangerously rough, and the sound of ocean waves crashing on rocks was loudly heard. It was getting darker and colder. We knew we wouldn't sail tonight.

"Abdo and Linda are hungry," said Haya. "We have only half a bottle left. We have nothing for later."

We ran out of water; we used most of it making milk for the toddlers. Amer, Mohamed, Othman, and I looked around for water bottles thrown on the ground, and we found many. They all contained some drops of water. We collected all the bottles we could find and got an amount of water that filled almost half a bottle.

Amer called the smuggler in Istanbul again. "OK, we will spend the night here, but we don't have water," he said. "We need to make milk for the kids, and there is no water. Many other families have kids as well. How would you like it if your children were here?"

"All right, I will send someone to bring you water, but this is the last time you call me. I have other things to take care of!"

Apparently, other things were more important than hundreds of people on an island with no water. We were but cargo to him.

After a while, one of the smugglers told us that he would drive to a village to get us some water and food. He came back two hour later with a few boxes of water, bread, and tomatoes.

The second he laid the boxes down, the Afghani guys raided. They carried the boxes and ran away. I tried to snatch a bottle of water from a box, but I got pushed to the ground.

I looked around to see if my brothers could get some water, but they were empty-handed. Within a minute, there was nothing left.

The families got nothing. Most of the families were Syrian, while there were only two or three Afghani families. We gathered ourselves and went to talk to the guys to give us some water and food, but they refused. The kids were starving, and the easy way wouldn't work. We tried to take a box of water by force, but we had to back down when they pulled out pocket knives on us.

With no other choice, we listened to the hunger cries of Abdo and Linda for a whole hour before a Syrian man came to us carrying some digestive biscuits.

"I know they are kind of young to eat biscuits, but try grinding them and feed the toddlers."

Another Syrian man followed and handed us a half bottle of water. "I could sneak a bottle of water," he said. "I and my family drank half of it, but the crying of your toddlers broke our hearts. Here, make them some milk. It will do."

We couldn't thank them enough. The toddlers got to eat and sleep after hours of hunger.

Three hours later, we saw someone coming out of the fog. It was the guy who fought with the smuggler and wanted to go back. A man walked up to him and asked why he had come back.

"We walked for hours and saw nothing but trees and stone," the man said. "There is no village near here. We gave up the idea of going back to Istanbul. The only option we had was taking the rubber boat."

It had been more than eight hours since we had last drank water. Our throats were dry and sore. Out of the bottle cap, each of us took a small sip, and we saved a little amount of water for the toddlers' next meal. We had plenty of food in our bags, but we had no appetite to eat any.

"Amer, call Ezz and ask him how the situation is in Izmir," I said.

"I tried five minutes ago. His phone is still out of coverage."

His phone battery must have died, I thought. We all had the same feeling, but no one wanted to talk about it. It was bedtime, except there was no bed. We put tree branches below us and used our clothes as a mattress.

"Guys, watch out for scorpions. I just killed one," yelled a guy in an unbothered tone of voice.

"Nice! Scorpions. Very nice!" said Othman sarcastically.

We had already seen many types of insects, but a scorpion was no joke. We were six people and two toddlers lying in less than four square meters under the trees. We slept on each other's legs and carried the toddlers on our chests to keep them warm and away from insects.

Hundreds of people were on the island, yet the atmosphere was terrifyingly quiet. Only the sound of cockroaches and the ghostly howling of the wind were heard. I had difficulty sleeping. I woke up every five minutes to change my sleep position from Mohamad's leg to Amer's during the hour I slept.

I felt something crawling on my arm. *Scorpion* was the first thing my brain thought of. I panicked and checked my arm to find a little flatworm crawling on it. I used my mobile screen light to check if there were any scorpions on my brothers; thankfully, there weren't. But Abdo and Othman weren't there.

I heard whispers. I got up carefully so as to avoid puncturing my head with a branch. I saw some people sitting around a campfire. Othman was there sitting on a rock holding Abdo, who was wrapped up in a light blanket. Sleeping wasn't that attractive, so I joined them.

There wasn't much talking going on. Everyone sat quietly except for one busy guy who was going around looking for something that we had no clue about.

"Hey, look up!" said Othman.

I looked up at the sky, and my jaw dropped instantly. I was completely lost. The black before me had a velvet quality. It was dark but glowing with hundreds of thousands of sparkling and shimmering stars. The sky was so spacious, it had no edges, yet it was crowded with falling stars, like a large hand had tossed diamond dust into the sky. I lost the silver moon while counting the stars.

How great is the universe and how small are we?

"Hell yeah! I found it," said the guy who was going around distracting my meditation. He was holding an empty can of tuna. He put it on the fire, poured in some water till it started boiling, threw the water away, then added new water and pulled out a coffee bag.

"Who wants some coffee?" he offered.

"Are you going to make coffee in that?" one guy asked.

"Yeah. I sterilized it."

"Whatever. I am not gonna say no to coffee."

He used a little stick to stir the coffee and passed the can to the guys, and everyone took a sip of it. It was a kind invitation, but I declined. I was not a big fan of coffee, especially when served in a tuna can.

We got into a long conversation, mostly about the journey and Europe. The name of the guy who made the coffee was Yazan. He looked to be the oldest among us. He had a skinny face and a black goatee.

"So, Yazan, what about you?" a guy asked. "Why do you want to go to Europe?"

"Why do I want to go to Europe? You should ask why would I *not*," he corrected him. "When I was in Aleppo, I got arrested due to the similarity of names. I spent three years and two months in jail. One thousand, one hundred, and fifty-five days. I suffered every single day, every hour, and every minute. I got raped hundreds of times … sometimes twice a day. When I tried to resist, they pulled out my fingernails."

I looked down at his fingers and got immediate goosebumps. I felt my hair standing up under my clothes.

"Not to mention the bruises all over my body and my broken ribs. They simply tried to kill me slowly. Every day, a small piece of me died. But my soul didn't. I wished nothing but death. I wanted to die, I tried to kill myself, but I couldn't. I begged others to kill me, but they were afraid of the consequences. Every night in the five-metre room which held ten people, I thought of my parents. I thought of the day I would get to see them." He closed his eyes and took a deep breath. When he opened them, they were glowing in pain. "They were dead."

After a needed pause, he continued. "My father died one year after my detention. My mother couldn't bear the loss of her son and husband and followed him after four months. All the time I spent I thought they were alive, waiting for me. None of my brothers were in Syria when I got out. One had emigrated to Lebanon, one to Egypt, and the other to Jordan. In those three years, the whole world changed. I wish that my life had stopped for three years, but it kept going and got only worse. So tell me, why should I stay? I am already dead inside and have nothing to lose. There are only two options now: either I drown in this sea or reach Europe and start a new life. Both solutions are fine for me."

He finished telling his story, and calmness prevailed.

Even though I had heard many similar stories before, such stories cannot be just heard. They are felt every time they are told. I tried to say something to him, but what could I say? *I'm sorry? It is going to be better?* That was the last thing he wanted to hear. No words and no actions were good enough to ease his past. We just sat there gazing at the sky.

"Sorry for telling such a story at such a time. Stupid me," said Yazan, breaking the silence. "Anyway, you are still young, and you still have time to study and work and start your lives all over again. For now, we all need to get some sleep, and hopefully, we will be able to take the rubber boat tomorrow."

How ironic. We hoped to go through the sea, the very thing we were terrified of.

Before going back to our den, I took one last glance at the sky. I lay down on Othman's leg and placed Abdo on my chest.

He lost everything: hope, faith, and his family. Drowning is our biggest fear, but for him, it is a solution. Inshallah—if God wills—we will make it to Greece safely in the morning. Once we reach Greece, everything will be fine. But what if we had to stay one more night here?

Before I realized, it was 04:00, and sleepiness overwhelmed my thoughts.

5
A Battle with the Sea
"We are gonna die!"

Monday/12-10-2015/06:10

"Wake up!"

"Give me my bag!"

"Linda is with me."

"Let's go, everybody. We are moving now!"

I found myself standing up before rubbing my sleepless eyes or shedding the sleep from my brain, but I had to get rid of the branches before they dug deeper holes in my body.

"Come on, Mohi," said Mohammad while picking up the bags.

I wore my jacket (which I'd used as a pillow), carried my bag, and followed along with the crowd. We walked down to the stony shore. The two smugglers were unboxing the rubber boats and the engines, and five minutes later, the first rubber boat was inflated and launched into the sea. I tried to grab a rubber boat with my brothers, but some Afghani guys snatched it from us by force. The same thing happened with other Syrian families.

"Get your act together!" a Syrian man shouted. "We won't get a chance to leave this damn island if we don't work together."

He was right. There were around two hundred Afghani guys and only five rubber boats left.

We gathered as a group and rushed to a rubber boat, but a gang of Afghani guys jumped on it before we got to it. We tried to grab it, but they called their friends who came and forced us back aggressively. It was the last boat.

We complained to the smuggler, who was busy unboxing the engines.

"All the boats were taken by Afghani people, and not a single Syrian person could get on a rubber boat," we told him. "We tried to get one, but they clashed with us. This is not fair."

He headed to the large group of Afghanis who were inflating the last rubber boat by jumping on a manual air pump.

"Hey, you! Leave this rubber boat. It is for the Syrians," said the smuggler. But he was ignored. He pulled out his pistol and shot a bullet into the air.

"I said, leave the goddamn boat, you piece of trash!"

"Hey! Calm down! We don't want the Turkish coastguard to find out about us!" said Amer.

"Then you better move fast!" said the smuggler.

The Afghani guys backed off and climbed and held onto other rubber boats that were already in the water. Most of them didn't have life jackets. Each rubber boat was boarded by over sixty people stacked over one another.

We took over the boat and continued inflating it. Meanwhile, the smuggler was filling the engine with diesel. It was half filled and looked ancient. It didn't seem to be working, but he said it would be fine. To be honest, *fine* was not the word people risking their lives wanted to hear.

"So, who will drive the boat?" asked the smuggler.

No one answered. No one wanted to take such responsibility.

"We don't have time to waste. The coastguard might appear at any second. Who will drive?"

"I'll drive it," said the man who had argued with the smuggler and tried to leave the island with his family.

"Good. Your name?" the smuggler asked.

"Laith."

"Did you drive a rubber boat before?"

"No," Laith admitted.

"OK, here is how," said the smuggler. "You need to grab the steering handle gently; you don't want to grab it so hard. By moving the handle to the left and the right, you can control the boat direction. Is everything clear?"

"Yes, I guess."

After a thirty-second presentation, we put on our life jackets and installed the engine, but still we were not ready. We had to carry the rubber boat to the water and keep a twenty-metre distance from the stony shore so that the propellers of the engine didn't hit the rocks.

We are doing this, we are taking the rubber boat.

The second my foot touched the water, I shuddered. My knees were shaking, my blood ran cold, and my breath became heavy. I was in the sea.

The guys jumped in the water and climbed into the boat. However, it wasn't as easy for the families. Twenty metres away from shore, the water was deep enough that we had to swim to reach the rubber boat. I, my brothers, and two other guys, including Yazan, helped the women and children get on the boat.

"Why are you sitting on the boat? Come back here and help the families! The rubber boat won't move until everyone is on it," Yazan rebuked the guys who left the women behind. Some went back to help while others stayed on the boat to give them a hand to climb it. Amer carried Linda on his head so that the water didn't reach her, while another guy carried Abdo. Mohamad was helping a random mother with her kids, and I was helping Haya.

The water was so deep that it reached our throats. One minute in the water, and we knew that moving with life jackets on wasn't an easy task. They tied our movement and kept on pulling us backwards, as the water was moving. They were simply an impediment.

I reached the boat with Haya and got help from two guys on board. The boat was slippery, and climbing it was a struggle.

I looked back at my brothers and had to yell so they could hear, "Do you need help?"

"No, stay there, we are coming," Mohamad yelled back.

Because of the rough movement of people, the boat was getting away from the shore. Haya's eyes were looking out for her kids anxiously. Amer finally reached the boat, and Haya stole Linda from him. I helped Amer get on the boat and took Abdo from the guy who had carried him.

Othman was helping Ghaithaa climb into the boat, but she kept on slipping.

"Here, put your foot on my shoulder and climb," said Othman.

She did as she was told and could finally get on the boat. She looked back but couldn't see Othman.

"Othman! Where are you!"

He had slipped under the rubber boat when she pushed herself on his shoulder. Seconds later, he freed himself and floated to the surface.

"These life jackets are … are fake … they don't help at all …"

Mohammad was the last to join us. After everyone settled down, the smuggler swam to our boat.

"Guys, throw away all of your baggage. You need to reduce the weight of the boat," said the smuggler as he started throwing the bags out of the boat.

We were over fifty people in a rubber boat designed to carry fifteen people. Having extra weight on it wouldn't be a bright idea.

"Please, my son, throw your bag away," said a woman who looked at me nervously.

There were only clothes and food in my backpack; my phone and passport were in a little cross-body bag. I wouldn't risk my life for some food. I threw my backpack into the water. Everybody else did the same. We only kept a small bag that contained diapers and powdered milk for the toddlers.

The smuggler started the engine while giving the driver more instructions. The noise was so loud I couldn't hear what he was saying, but I could feel the boat moving. He drove the boat for about thirty metres and then told the driver, Laith, to take control from now on. Then he jumped in the water and swam back to shore to help the last Afghani boat, which seemed to have issues.

Our boat wasn't steady, and Laith looked nervous. His hands were shaking, and his forehead was sweating. I couldn't blame him. He was responsible for the lives of more than fifty people, including his wife and two children.

I sat at the edge of the boat next to Haya, who had Linda on her lap. Mohamad was sitting opposite us. Othman and Ghaithaa were in the middle, while Amer was holding Abdo and sitting beside Yazan.

Ten minutes later, we were far away from the shore. The depth of the sea was so great and dark. People were praying and reading the Quran out loud. Gradually, the voices were becoming louder. Even though there was nothing to do but pray at that moment, it became so tense, and it was affecting Laith's focus.

"People, please shut up, just stop," said Mohamad strictly. "The driver is stressed enough. Let him focus. You can pray with your hearts."

The voices became quieter. Still, there was some mumbling.

As we drove farther into the sea, the last Afghani boat that launched after ours passed us. It wasn't too fast, but Laith was driving slowly and anxiously. No one objected. Moving slowly was a much better option than going fast and risking that the boat would flip over.

"Look! It's the Turkish coastguard!" A guy pointed his finger at a cutwater boat with a Turkish flag.

I hope they don't …

"What are you doing?" said Mohamad to the guy next to him, who was holding a pocketknife.

"I will pierce the boat if the Turkish coastguard comes near us so that they don't return us to Turkey!" the guy said.

"Throw the knife away," Mohamad growled, but the guy didn't listen. "If you don't throw the knife away right this second, I swear to God, I will throw you into the sea!"

Everyone shouted at the guy ferociously until he was forced to throw the knife away.

My eyes were stuck on the Turkish coastguard ship. It wasn't moving.

"I bet they have been bribed and are collaborating with the smugglers," said Yazan.

Amer holding Abdo and taking a photo in the rubber boat

Three hours passed. There was no talking. The waves were hitting the rubber boat, transient yet always there as a reminder to not relax. I had been seeing nothing but seawater for hours. My brain started composing a drowning scenario.

What should I do if the boat sinks? Who should I help? My brothers can take care of themselves, but the toddlers are so young. Should I rescue Linda or Abdo? Haya or Ghaithaa? Or the nearest person to me?

What am I even saying? Will I be able to rescue myself in the first place? I am not that good at swimming. I cannot recall the last time I swam.

Will we drown? Will anyone notice? Or will we just fade away from this world? Will my family and friends know that I drowned?

Out of the blue, the engine stopped. The scenario in my head seemed to be turning into a reality.

"What is the matter? Did it run out of the diesel?" asked Amer.

"I don't know, but the engine is extremely hot," replied Laith.

"What do we do?" asked one man.

"I am afraid that we have to give the engine a rest to cool down," said Laith.

"Amer, check out the GPS so we don't lose the track," said Mohamad.

After a couple of minutes of waiting, grey clouds were easily seen approaching and swirling in a tumult from afar. The wind wasn't as gentle as before; it was getting stronger. The boat started to sway and ended up circling around.

"My brother, please drive back to Turkey. I don't want my children to die. Please go back," a woman said in a shaky voice.

"It is going to be OK. Don't worry. We are just resting the engine a bit," said Laith in an attempt to calm her and everyone down.

The weather gradually worsened until five-foot waves were crashing into the boat. One wave was more than enough to fill the boat with plenty of water. The shouting got higher, and the boat started to spin around faster.

Ghaithaa was crying in silence.

Othman asked her, "Ghaithaa? What is the matter?"

"My legs," she said. "I can't feel them."

She had a kid on her lap and another woman sitting on her legs. It had been more than three hours without us being able to make a single movement to avoid unbalancing the boat.

"The Turkish coastguard is coming towards us!" shouted a guy.

"Are they coming to help?" asked another guy anxiously.

"No, I have seen videos. They will sink our boat!" shrieked a woman.

"Run the engine!" shouted Othman at Laith.

Laith attempted to pull out the engine rope and almost fell out. "I need help!" he shouted.

A man sitting next to Laith held him to keep him from falling out. Laith made many attempts, but the engine was not responding at all.

The Turkish coastguard boat was more advanced, thus so fast. It was approaching us quickly. When it reached us, it started going around in circles, causing our fragile rubber boat to lose its balance. They were trying to sink us. The extreme and unsteady movements of the boat pushed me to throw up.

"We are gonna die!" a woman cried out in horror.

A coastguardsman had a long iron stick with a sharp end. He started piercing the boat spitefully. His eyes were burning in hatred. "Die! Die! Die!" he shouted.

He … he is willing to kill us! But why? For what reason? How can a human be able to waste the lives of more than fifty people? Why does he detest us? Is it hatred that motivates him? No way he is just doing his job and following orders. Was this what the agreements between Turkey and Europe to limit illegal immigration was all about?

One guy tried to snatch the iron stick but got hit by it on his head and started to bleed immediately. The Turkish coastguard left us then to sink slowly and went after the other rubber boats.

It was what I feared. They had waited for us to reach the centre of the sea, to drive away from the Turkish shore so we could neither go back to Turkey nor reach Greece.

"Water! There is water in the boat! The boat is leaking water!" a terrified shout came out of the woman sitting next to me.

I looked down at the boat, making sure I was not moving too fast so I didn't cause more imbalance to the boat. There was indeed water getting in. Even though maintaining the boat's balance was our priority, everyone started to freak out.

"Calm down, calm down!" shouted a man.

I saw Othman's lips moving, but I couldn't figure out what he was trying to say. Women were bawling and sobbing while holding their babies, who were in extreme fear, not understanding what was going on.

"Please God, we don't want to die. We don't want our children to drown. Please, God, save us!" a woman prayed.

"Amer, Amer, my phone isn't working. Contact the Greek coastguard!" shouted Mohammad.

Amer gave Abdo to another guy and pulled out his phone.

"Amer, don't! Don't leave Abdo!" clamoured Haya, but she couldn't be heard.

"Help us! We are drowning! Send help!" Amer shouted. His phone had been put in a plastic bag to keep it from getting wet, and he couldn't hear clearly. He ended the call and sent a message of our location.

Some guys started to take the water out of the boat using their bare hands. Others took off their life jackets and shirts and use the shirts to keep the water from gushing in. I looked around not knowing what to do. All of a sudden, I saw something that made my heart beat even harder.

"The Greek island, I see it! I can see it!" I shouted out loud so everyone could hear me.

Yazan stuck half of his body out of the boat and used his mouth as a suction pump to cause the diesel to move around to help the engine work.

"Ughhh!" We heard a noise. The engine worked!

"Hold on to the boat! We are going as fast as possible!" shouted Laith.

Yazan succeeded in starting the engine, but he had swallowed some diesel and threw up. Knowing that we were going to drown anyway, closing the distance between us and the Greek shore was the best thing Laith could come up with.

We were moving so fast that the boat was jumping on the surface of the water and climbing up the waves. I jumped out of the boat and landed on the edge. A woman grabbed me back to her lap.

"Hold on to my leg, Mohi!" squeaked Haya.

The guy who was sitting next to Mohamad fell out of the boat.

"There is nothing we can do! In seconds, we will all join him," Yazan interrupted the guy who seemed to think about rescuing the guy who fell.

Black smoke was coming out of the engine, and the engine completely died before the boat sank. Everyone stayed still for a long second and wondered what to do next. The Greek island was around two kilometres away.

"Hello! Dad!" A guy drew our attention while sending a farewell voice message to his father in Syria. "I am sorry I didn't tell you before. I just didn't want you to worry about me. I am in the sea. I am going to die. Please forgive me for everything!"

A woman cried out, "My kids! my kids!"

Everyone was freaking out. It was the moment we had all feared. Now, we were living it.

"Calm down, everyone!" shouted Yazan. "The Greek island is near. Try to swim to it!" He jumped in the water with some other guys.

"What do we do?!" I looked at my brothers, terrified.

"We will have to swim—stick to each other," said Amer.

People were hesitant, but time was passing by.

Dear God. I jumped into the briny grey water, and so did my brothers and their wives. Othman was holding Ghaithaa's hand to keep the waves from separating them. She looked miserably terrified. She wanted to cry, to express her feelings, but she only felt terror.

Amer was carrying Abdo on his head. The boy wasn't crying; he was in a state of shock, not knowing what was happening.

"Get your heads down!" Mohamad was shouting. Before I got the chance to do as he said or to understand why, a huge wave hit me from behind, knocking me down.

My head went down, and my legs were facing the surface. I hadn't moved my legs for four hours, and they felt like chunks of wood that were attached to my body. Luckily, I could make a turn and go back to the surface. I opened my mouth wide to gasp for air, but before I had the chance to do so, another vicious wave hit me and knocked me down again, dragging the air from my lungs.

Water gushed down into my lungs. I was going down so fast. I was kicking the water with my legs, but that only dragged me farther down.

Suddenly, I was in a war of survival. Yet everything was quiet. I couldn't hear anything—not even the loud hurricane of my own thoughts. It was a frightening stillness down there. The depth of the sea looked endless. It was so dark, and it was swallowing me.

I tried to scream, to shout, to beg, and to cry. My head was about to explode. The sea was my theatre, but everybody declined their invitations. Nobody was present to watch my show. Nobody saw me.

My sight was gradually becoming darker when a one-second flashback suddenly showed in my mind: I was playing and laughing with my cousins in my grandfather's house in Syria. Everything I'd learned about surviving dissolved from my brain.

My brain didn't show me the instructions I had learned in the swimming lessons when I was 7 years old. It didn't remind me of how strong and tough I thought I was. It didn't motivate me. Instead, it was busy sending signals to my organs to do whatever their job was.

It wasn't my brain that showed me the flashback; perhaps it was my soul. Being a child, surrounded by my family, and playing all day long with my cousins with nothing to worry about was the warmest thing my soul could afford to warm up my cold body. A memory I didn't think meant so much to me turned out to be all I ever wanted: to live peacefully, like the good old days.

I'd expected to drown, but I wasn't expecting it to happen this fast. I wasn't expecting my life to end in seconds. My muscles relaxed, and I was oddly calm for a moment. My heart began to give up its fight, and my body stopped altogether. Then everything slowly faded to black. For some reason, it didn't hurt like I thought it would. I wasn't panicking anymore. It was almost peaceful, actually.

Don't stop!

An inner order from myself to my soul brought me back to reality.

Don't stop!

Nobody but me could keep me safe. I had to do something. I had to save myself. This was my last-man-standing moment. This was me versus the great Mediterranean Sea. My soul, my heart, my brain, and my lifeless body listened to myself and started working together, started fighting to reach the watery grave surface.

As I kicked viciously through the water, I felt an intense pain in my thighs. My muscles had a spasm. Ignoring the pain, I continued making my way to the surface. I was surviving.

The surface was so close, yet so far away. It felt unreachable. I was about to faint. It felt like there hadn't been any air in my lungs for decades. My arms and legs were moving feebly.

Finally, I saw a hand. I knew whose hand it was. It was Othman's.

The bright orange colour of my life jacket made it easier for him to find me. He got a strong hold of my hand and pulled me back to the surface, back to the noisy boisterous world and out of that creepy silence.

The air was the very first thing I was seeking, but my breaths were agonizingly painful and terribly short. I was coughing and inhaling at the same time. I saw nothing, as there were oceans in my eyes. But I could hear Othman shouting, "Dive in!"

I knew what was coming, and I would never want to experience it again: another huge wave. I dived under to avoid it. I raised my head again to the surface and continued replacing the water in my lungs with air.

"Ghaithaa, keep moving your legs!" shouted Mohamad. He was holding another woman's hand.

"I am moving them, but they are sore," replied Ghaithaa in pain.

"Can you manage yourself now?" Othman asked me.

"Yes … I will be all right … go help Ghaithaa," I said while coughing.

"Take off your life jacket. It sucks," he said before swimming back to Ghaithaa.

All my movements were subtle. They rarely made any noise at all. It felt like I had spent hours under the surface, while in the real world, it was but seconds. I just woke myself up from the creepiest nightmare. Still, the fight wasn't over.

Haya was drifting away on the waves. She was keeping her face and Linda's face above the water; the child was holding strongly to her mother. I took off my fake life jacket, which had only one job and failed miserably at it, so I could move freely and swim to her.

"Haya, give Linda to me," I said.

"No! She will stay with me!" she replied.

"I will keep her safe."

"She will only be safe in my arms. I won't give her to anyone!" Haya insisted. Her maternal instinct had kicked in, and she wasn't even trusting me, Linda's uncle, to carry her daughter.

"We can't stay like this. We need to swim to the shore," shouted Amer with Abdo on his head.

It was challenging to swim in such rambunctious weather. The rain was becoming one with the unsteady waves. We swam slowly and carefully. Sometimes the waves pushed us closer to the island; other times, we were pulled away.

Thirty minutes of swimming and diving was more than enough to beat the hell out of us. Our bodies were screaming in pain. We wanted to rest, but we had to continue swimming. Otherwise, we would probably drown.

I heard a conversation between an old mother and her two kids. She seemed to surrender. She knew she wouldn't make it.

"I cannot move any longer!" the mother cried out to her son. "Hold your sister's hand. Never let go of her!"

"But Mom, don't leave us here, please!"

I wanted to tell the mother to stay strong, to hold on just for a little more. I wanted to shout, yet I was about to give up myself. Giving a motivational speech was the last thing I could do. It wasn't like in the movies. I was too busy staying alive.

"Go now! Reach the shore and ask for help. I will follow you. Just go with your sister!" She gave her son the final order.

We swam past her while she was trying to stay floating and coughing the water out of her mouth. Her son grabbed the hand of his younger sister, and the waves separated them from their mother.

The pain distracted me from everything around me. It didn't want to leave me. Every single muscle ached. My lips were frozen, and I wanted nothing but rest, even if it would cost me my life.

"I … I can no longer feel my body," I told my brothers.

"Let's just stay floating," said Othman.

"Wait, something is coming towards us. A boat!" yelled Ghaithaa, pointing with her eyes.

It was true! A rubber boat was picking Laith and his family out of the sea. It seemed to be heading towards us, but before it reached us, it drove back to shore, for it was filled with people.

"Oh my God! Thank God! Help is here!" yelled Haya happily. "They will come back for us. Hold on!"

We grabbed tightly to the treacherous sea, waiting for rescue. We had been many on the boat, but as I looked around me, only a few people shared the sea with me. They might have made it to shore safely. Or they might be under me.

I looked further and saw a sinking rubber boat full of Afghani people. I could hear nothing. It felt like watching a video with the sound off. They were experiencing the very same thing we had: death!

I followed a woman with my eyes trying desperately to stay on the surface, but she didn't seem to know how to swim. I kept on staring. I wanted to make sure she would come back to the surface. I kept on staring for minutes. She didn't come back to the surface. She drowned.

Probably nobody noticed her existence. Her life just ended. She couldn't survive as I had. She lost the fight. She moved to the underworld, the cold silent one.

A man wearing shorts and a tank top was approaching us using one of the rubber boats that had arrived safely.

"Here! Hand me the kids!" he told Amer and Haya.

He carried Abdo and Linda and handed them to the people who were already in the boat, then he continued to pull us from the sea along with the other people. While he was giving me his hand, he was busy searching for other people.

"Are there any people left here?" he asked.

"Yes, my mother!" cried out the little boy whose mother told him to take care of his sister.

"Where is she?" asked the man.

"I don't know. She said that she would follow me. She was resting in the water."

"All right, everyone, search for other people!" said the guy as he drove the boat to where the mother was.

"Mama! Mama!" called out the boy and his sister for their mother.

We were all looking out for the mother and other survivors. We kept on driving and searching for five minutes.

"Ma-Mama … Where are you mama? The help has arrived! Where are you?" The kid's voice started to tremble.

The guy who was driving gave the child a look of pity. The boat made a turn and headed to the Greek island.

"Where are you going? My mom is still here! I can't leave her!" shouted the boy out loud.

"I will come back for her, I promise. There are other people who need help at the moment. Otherwise, they will drown."

"I don't care! I need my mother! Now!" replied the boy in a rage.

People pulled the boy and his sister closer to them to calm them down while they were losing their minds.

We got near the Greek island and saw volunteers from the Red Cross, hopping and waving their hands, yelling that we had made it. I cried—this time, tears of exhilarating joy.

We couldn't contain our happiness and waved back heartily as we were slowly but surely reaching the Greek island. We did it! We reached the stony shore, and the volunteers rushed to the boat to help us.

Haya and Ghaithaa got off first, and we handed Abdo and Linda to them. Never have I wished so much for land, to feel the hard and steady soil of safety.

"You are safe now! You are safe now!" yelled an old volunteer man in Arabic.

Happiness burst into my soul when I heard his words. We felt safe; we were safe. Mixed feelings caused tears of tragedy and happiness to run out of my eyes. It was the happiest moment, yet the most desperate.

A Syrian woman threw herself at a volunteer woman, and they both cried emotionally.

"Thank you, God. Thank you for allowing us to reach the shore safely," said the Syrian woman in Arabic.

"You are safe now, I promise you. You are safe now," replied the volunteer in English.

They didn't understand each other, but they felt each other. Language wasn't necessary for that scenario. Feelings played the main role.

My thighs were twitching, and I couldn't walk. I crawled away from the shore to a rock and lay on my back. The guy who'd rescued us turned on the engine again and drove back to the sea to rescue more people.

Amer and Haya followed a volunteer to get dry clothes and mashed fruits bags for Abdo and Linda. Mohammad was hugging Ghaithaa while she was looking at the people in the sea and crying. Othman sat next to me. He said nothing; he has never been good at expressing his feelings. I expected him to sympathize with me, but it was very likely that he wanted me to sympathize with him. I never knew. We just sat there looking at the people celebrating life.

Amer finally got a signal and called my parents. He couldn't hold his tears.

"Mom! We reached Greece! We survived!"

"Thank God! Thank God you are safe! I prayed all day and all night, and my prayers weren't in vain! I love you, sweetheart!" blubbered my mother.

I was watching everything around me. I didn't know what to feel. I was glad but felt miserable watching people suffering in the sea while I was on land. We all had the same nightmare, but not everyone could wake up. Many people died around me without me being able to move a muscle. I saw them drowning, fading away slowly after they lost their fight. No one would know their names. No one would know their stories but the sea.

Our story wasn't over, but for thousands, their story had met its end in the water.

At least we had passed the hardest part of the journey. That's what we thought, anyway. I wish it was true.

6
Unforgettable Sorrow
"He is still not answering"

"In twenty minutes, buses will come to transfer the families to a temporary place. Guys will have to walk," said a volunteer of the Red Cross.

Walking was no problem at all. On the contrary, we were more than happy to walk and feel the land beneath our feet. Amer, Haya, Ghaithaa, and the toddlers waited for the bus while I, Othman, and Mohamad followed the paved road to where the families were taken.

I had promised my friends Hamza and Bedir I would inform them as soon as I reached Greece. I pulled my phone out from my cross-body bag and pressed the power button. It showed a white screen for a second and shut down after. I knew it was dead.

For some reason, I wasn't sad or upset. I had just survived, and a dead phone wasn't a big deal. Mohamad's phone wasn't working either. Only Othman's phone was fine.

We reached the peak of the island where we could see the whole spacious sea. The weather wasn't getting any better. Gigantic dark rainy clouds shot lightning at the sea, followed by thunder. Thankfully, there were no rubber boats in the sea, for no one would ever escape such a vicious storm.

Along the road, we met many volunteers who came to help us, the refugees, and save as many as they could. Whenever we passed by, they would smile at us and greet us. They truly made us feel welcomed.

"Hello, guys! Need water?" a driver asked us as he stopped his car near us.

"Yes, please!" I answered.

"Well, I have only one bottle left. Can you share it?"

"Of course!"

Even though I had swallowed a gallon of seawater, it had made me even more thirsty. We decided to take a rest and enjoy the water.

Amer and the rest passed by in a van. We continued walking, and after an hour, we got to the place where the families had gathered. The Red Cross was present, handing out cheese sandwiches and water. We were told that buses were on their way to drive us to a temporary camp. A while later, two buses arrived,

Othman, me and Mohamad
after surviving the sea.

and we formed lines to get on them. When I first sank into my seat, I recognized how tired I was, but looking at the trees embracing the road tightly from every direction was a treat that I needed.

One hour later, we reached the camp. At first glance, it wasn't what I expected. We stood in a line, and I examined the camp's poor condition. I had seen camps on the news before, but being in a camp was a whole different story.

The camp was separated from the highway by a chain-link fence. It had six small tents that could fit one or two families and two enormous tents that could fit around 150 people each. We got yellow cards from volunteers, and we were told that we could use the cards to get food.

Our feet made an unpleasant muddy sound on our way to the large tent. People were carrying their stuff and getting on the same buses we got off from. I went to investigate and asked the driver where those people were going. He asked for the colour of my card.

"Those who have yellow cards will move to the second camp tomorrow at 06:00. Today, we are taking the blue cards."

We had no idea what to do or where to go, and apparently, this wasn't the only camp, as I had thought.

There was a mountain of mattresses and blankets in the corner of the shelter. We grabbed three big mattresses and arranged them next to each other. Before we settled down, we did like the others and went to get some food from two small tents that the volunteers used to prepare sandwiches. After showing the yellow cards, we were given a cheese sandwich, a plastic cup of milk, and a banana.

While we were eating, Laith and his family entered the tent carrying food and searching for a place to sit.

"Isn't that the rubber boat driver?" Ghaithaa asked, pointing.

"Here! Come and join us!" Amer waved at him.

Othman and I grabbed them a mattress and put it next to ours. By the time we finished eating, the tent was almost full of people.

"Thanks a lot for taking responsibility. You are very brave," said Mohamad.

"Wait, who is brave? Me? Man, my hands didn't stop shaking," he giggled.

"No one blames you. I would never have been able to do that. By the way, where were you living before coming to Greece?" asked Mohamad.

"I lived in Idlib in Syria. I spent one week in Turkey waiting to get an answer from the smugglers," Laith replied.

"So you didn't live in Turkey before? I am sorry, but why did you decide to go to Europe?" Othman asked curiously.

"Like every other person, I don't have a place to live in."

"Why? What happened?" I asked.

"It is a long story, but I don't think we will be having a meeting anytime soon," he giggled. "I lived together with my brother and his family in a small apartment in Idlib in Syria. One day, I, my wife, Sarah, and my son, Adam, who is 10 years old, went to the market to buy groceries. While we were out of the apartment, the sky rained missiles as two airplanes bombed the city. I carried my son, held Sarah's hand, and ran to the unknown, but nowhere was safe. People were freaking out and running for their lives. A bomb fell just a couple of metres away from us, tearing a man's body apart."

Sarah wept as she recalled that day, and the freckles stood out on her pale face.

"What about your brother?" asked Othman.

Before Laith continued, he took a deep breath. "My brother? When the bombing stopped, everyone was looking for dead bodies of their relatives and injured people to save. I ran back to the apartment and found nothing but stones. The entire building was down. I climbed up the rubble and threw rocks away. I was screaming his name, 'Ahmad! Ahmad!'

"I heard crying. It was his 8-year-old little son, Yosef. He was under the rubble, and I could see only his foot. Sarah and I removed the rubble upon his body and could luckily pull him out. I continued to look for my brother and his wife desperately until I heard a faint sound. It was my brother. I dug with my bare hands and saw his arm."

Laith's voice cracked so hard, and he had to stop and pull himself together before continuing. "He was under a huge rock that I couldn't move. No matter how hard I tried, the rock didn't move. I was shouting for help. Everybody was busy trying to save their beloved ones. I felt so lonely; not a single person in the world could help me save my brother. I never felt this helpless. After one hour, three guys came to help me move the rock, but it was too late. His upper body was completely smashed. He was gone. I wish I could understand what he was trying to tell me. To hear his last words."

"His wife couldn't be found. Her body just disappeared. It is a miracle that Yosef survived," said Sarah, rubbing Yosef's head gently. "He has no one to take care of him but us, and it is our responsibility to raise him. He is as precious as my son Adam. Ever since that day, Yosef can barely talk. That day had a huge impact on both his soul and personality."

"If I knew the land was safer than the sea, I would never have put Yosef and my family at such risk," said Laith. "It is funny to say, but that sea was a hundred times safer than our home."

There are endless types of grief and sorrow, but losing a brother under the rubble before your eyes must have been the worst. I wondered if I would have given up if I was in Laith's shoes. I doubted I would. Just hours ago, my brother saved me from drowning. If one of my brothers was the one to drown, I would never have forgiven myself. Ever.

My senses were taut with concentration while listening to Laith's story, but by the time he had finished, I realized how jammed and noisy the tent had become. Syrian, Afghani, Iraqi, and Persian families and guys had conquered the camp, and there weren't enough mattresses or blankets for everyone. It was like an international festival—an undesirable concert that was played by a crowd who didn't know the lyrics, let alone the high note that no one but the crying kids could sing.

Haya was putting the toddlers to sleep, and I could hardly hear her telling me to ask the volunteers to clean the milk bottles with hot water. I took the bottles and walked happily to a less noisy world. I ambled up to a volunteer in a tent.

"Excuse me, could you please wash these milk bottles for the toddlers?"

"Yeah, sure! How was your trip?" asked the volunteer.

"It wasn't easy. We weren't treated as humans," I replied.

"I am sorry to hear that. But you made it alive to Greece, and that is something you should be happy for," she said with a smile.

"You are right. Thanks for reminding me. I don't know what to say. You could be at home drinking coffee under your comfy blanket but you decided to come out here in this cold to help people you've never met before."

"Don't worry about us!" she said. "We are more than happy to be able to help those who are in need, and I am sure many people also want to help you. For now, you need to take good care of yourself and be safe. Unfortunately, on Lesbos, this island, the next camps are not as good as this camp, so I hope you don't meet any difficulties."

Aren't as good as this camp? Is this camp any good in the first place?

I wanted to ask about the other camps, but I didn't. She wasn't there to chat with me; she was there to help. She handed me the bottles. She had cleaned them with hot water and filled them with milk.

The tent was raucous. People were coming in and going out, and the children were running around playing and shouting. I gave Haya the bottles and rushed out to watch the sunset alone. When it was dark, the camp became a bit quieter.

In the end, everyone was exhausted after the fancy trip on the yacht. I had to go back to the tent after the cold seeped into my fingers and spread painfully throughout my torso. I sat on the mattress. Before I lay my body down, a guy squatted down next to me and asked in Arabic, "Hi, do you want me to drive you to the next camp?"

It was the same guy who got us out of the sea and drove us to the Greek island. I hadn't expected to see him again. I told him that I needed to wake my older brother up. I gave Amer a nudge.

"Good evening," the man said to Amer. "If you want, I can drive you to the next camp so you don't need to wait for the bus, but don't tell anyone. I don't want problems."

"Thanks, but can you give us some time to discuss? I mean, you just came out of nowhere and offered to drive us. What is your name?"

Salam Aldeen from Team Humanity helping refugees on Lesbos island.

"Of course. My name is Salam Aldeen. I can speak Arabic, but I live in Denmark. After I saw the photo of Alan Kurdi, the 3-year-old toddler, I was convinced that watching was never enough and decided to do something for the refugees. Think about it, and I'll be waiting for your answer outside. Otherwise, I need to ask another family if they want a ride."

Amer was hesitant. He talked to Laith, who said, "Yeah, that guy just talked to me too, but I prefer not to trust anybody. I've heard many stories about organ trade, so I said no."

Amer called my father to ask him for advice, while I asked the volunteers if they knew this guy.

"Good that you asked, just give me a minute," said the volunteer. She came back and said, "Yes, you can trust that guy. He is working with us."

I went back to Amer and told him that the guy was a volunteer as well. Amer was still hesitant, and my father said that it would be better to be in a group of people. Anyways, the buses would come in about seven hours. We decided to stay. Salam had already spoken with another family.

"By the way, did Ezz call them?" I asked when Amer was off the phone.

"He rang them, but there was a clicking noise during the call, and they couldn't hear him. His phone might be water-damaged."

Or …

It was time to sleep. I lay down, but there was a war in my head. Hours ago, I was in the middle of the sea. I couldn't stop thinking of what had happened to me and others, about Laith's story, and about the many people who had gone through the same story or worse. Somehow, I felt guilty to survive the sea while others couldn't. Maybe I was dealing with survivor's syndrome.

My throat was sore. It felt like I had swallowed a stone and it got stuck. My body was tired, but my soul was drained.

Despite the unbearable din and the nonstop coughing, my heavy eyes finally closed.

Tuesday/13-10-2015/05:50

Almost everyone in the camp was awake. We waited outside the shelter for the buses, carrying a small bag that had milk and diapers. The buses didn't take long. We showed the driver our yellow cards and were ready to go, but unexpectedly, we got off after ten minutes. We had arrived at the next camp.

There were a couple of kiosks selling food and coffee near the highway and many tents that could be seen from afar. We waited with Laith and his family for a volunteer to guide us on what to do. No one showed up.

We walked around the camp looking for anyone who could help us and give us some information. We found ourselves surrounded by many small flat-pack shelters placed close to each other. Fortunately, we saw a Syrian family. We asked them what we should do.

"First of all," the man of the family told us, "you need to search for an empty shelter to stay in. Only a few are left."

"Is it possible that we are going to spend the night here?" asked Amer.

"Most likely yes. After this camp, you will go to a police station where you can get the white card."

"The white card? What is that?" Amer asked.

"As I understood, it is a protection applicant's card that is valid for six months," answered the man. He pointed his finger. "You see that place where people are standing in lines? You need to go there and get a number that you will use to get to the police station. I and my family got numbers and are leaving this camp today."

We thanked him and did as he told us to do. After half an hour of searching, we finally found an empty shelter to stay in. Amer, Mohamad, Othman, and Laith went to get more information on how to get numbers, and I stayed with the women and kids. It was hot outside, and the shelter was completely empty, with nothing to sit on but gravel and cartons.

Mohamad came back after a short time and told Ghaithaa to follow him. The men's line was too long, unlike the women's. We waited two hours before everyone came back sweating.

"Did you get a number?" I asked.

"The lines were cancelled. There won't be any numbers given today. We have to wait until tomorrow."

Linda and Abdo in the shelter

That wasn't what I wanted to hear. It was 08:00.

We sat on the ground with nothing to do. Amer seemed to be making a phone call.

"Who are you calling?" I asked.

"Ezz. He is still not answering. I am afraid he drowned in the sea." Amer said what we all denied and avoided saying.

"Don't say that!" I said, trying to persuade myself that Ezz was still alive. "Maybe his phone got wet and stopped working like mine." Drowning was a possibility, but I wanted to believe the other possibility: that he was still alive. Yet a hurricane of pessimism was howling in my head. We hadn't heard from Ezz in two days.

After hours, we saw people gathering in the same place where one got a number. Amer, Othman, Ghaithaa, and Laith went there quickly to investigate and stood in line. Only a few people were in front of them.

"One family member is enough to get numbers for the family," instructed the security guard. "The other family members can go back to the shelters."

Ghaithaa and Othman returned to the shelter and waited with us. When it was Amer's turn, he told the officer how many we were, but they gave him only four numbers. They considered Mohamad and Ghaithaa an independent family, and they needed to be present in order to get a number. Amer tried to convince them that we were one family and came together, but they were not cooperative.

I was looking for Amer when he saw me. "Tell Mohamad and Ghaithaa to come here immediately!"

I ran back and told them to follow me, but a security guard was preventing more people from getting in. I explained what had happened but he refused to let us in. The line was too long, and only one security guard was managing it.

He got distracted by other people, and Mohamad and Ghaithaa sneaked in and rushed to Amer. Luckily, they got in and were given numbers after Amer proved we were a family.

Our numbers began with 843, while Laith and his family got numbers that began with 716. We were told that the buses would take those who had numbers between 700 and 900, and we were happy to leave the camp on the same day.

We waited for the buses on the highway, and shortly after, two buses came. The drivers called out for people who had numbers between 700 and 800. More buses were coming to pick up those who had numbers between 800 and 900.

Laith's family went first, and we agreed to meet at the police station. The buses were supposed to arrive in one hour. We waited for two hours, but no buses showed up. Yet there were many buses that some people took on their own.

Amer and I talked to a security guard, and he said that the buses should be here soon. He also said that if we went there by ourselves, we would be returned.

A large clothing store was on the other side of the highway, reminding us that we needed to change our salty clothes. They weren't wet anymore, but they caused itching. We didn't have much money, and we were only on the third day of the journey. We needed to use our money wisely. But the shop kept looking at us, and we couldn't resist the temptation. We bought comfy trousers for us, Haya, and Ghaithaa to move in freely, and Othman and I bought military T-shirts—not for camouflage, but because they were cheap and soft.

While we were waiting on the sidewalk, a Syrian guy approached us and said, "Hello! I just wanted to say that you don't need to wait here. You can take a bus to the police station for one euro. My friend went there and said that they don't ask about your number."

We weren't the only ones he spoke to. More people started taking buses to the police station.

"Should we go with the people or should we wait?" I asked.

"Let's wait. As the officer said, if we go by ourselves, they will send us back, and then we will have to wait on lines again to get new numbers," said Mohamad.

We hadn't had anything to eat since the day before, and the smell of the fast food made us crave it. We didn't know what was coming next or how long were we going to wait, so we bought three grilled cheese sandwiches that cost two euros each and cut them in halves.

"Hello! Hello! Do you need a SIM card? It is international," an elderly man said in Arabic.

Othman and Haya's phones were the only ones working besides Amer's, but they had Turkish SIM cards that didn't work in Europe. Amer had already bought one from Turkey, and it would be safer to get another SIM card in case we got separated, so Othman bought one.

"How long have you been here?" Amer asked the man.

"Well, I live in Greece, and I like to see the people of my country and talk to them."

"Nice to meet you," Amer said. "By the way, do you know about the police station? Should we wait or take the bus there?"

"Well, it is hot and I see you have toddlers, I don't think you need to wait. Don't tell anyone, but go. They won't send you back here."

People who had left on their own hadn't been returned. In the end, we decided not to wait anymore. We took the next bus to the police station, which was only ten minutes away from the camp. The first thing we saw after getting off the bus was two lines of people: one for Syrians and one for Iraqi and Afghani people. A volunteer was giving people a piece of paper. He got to us, and we showed him our numbers.

"Oh, no, you don't need these here. Here are your new numbers.

We had waited for six hours for nothing, and we felt kind of foolish for insisting on waiting, but things weren't going as we thought. We had a conversation with the guy in front of us about the white card, and we learned it was called an "international protection seeker's card" that would be issued with our personal details. We also found out that our next station was Athens, and we needed the white card to take a ferry there.

The police station was surrounded by a high chain-link fence with a gate and had a big yard. The line was moving very slowly—one step forward every ten minutes. Amer went with Linda to investigate the reason. Half an hour passed, and he hadn't come back. Othman went after him and saw him on the other side of the fence gate.

"Bring me all the passports," Amer told Othman. "Maybe one family member is enough."

We could finally get closer to the gate, but then the line stopped moving. An hour passed before a police officer showed up to inform us that we had to wait until they were done with the people who were already inside the gate.

We were standing in the boiling sun, and it was getting extremely hot. Abdo couldn't handle the heat and had been crying for half an hour straight. We tried wiping his face with water to cool him, but he didn't stop crying. "I know this is hard" and "it is going to be OK" wouldn't make him stop. He was nearly out of breath.

I ran to call for help, and a volunteer from the Red Cross saw me. I told her about Abdo, and we both ran back to him. She carried Abdo to a small tent, and Haya followed her. They washed his face with water and gave him sedative medicine to calm him down.

When a baby cries, a mother's heart breaks. That is what I believe, and Haya's heart was indeed broken. She couldn't help but burst into tears. The volunteer stayed with Haya until she calmed down and Abdo fell asleep, and filled the bottles with milk as well.

When Haya came back with Abdo, there was no longer a line but a gathering around the gate. We weren't going to stand in the middle with Abdo, so I, Haya, and Ghaithaa walked away and sat on the dirt. We stayed near the gate prepared in case they opened it.

"You have to stand in a line. Otherwise, none will get in!" barked a police officer after two hours.

Othman took the lead and tried to organize the crowd with another guy, but no one listened to them. Instead, people started to scramble, and some guys climbed the fence and jumped to the other side of the gate. The situation became more chaotic.

A volunteer then came and wrote numbers on our hands in an attempt to organize the crowd. Once again, the numbers we got when we first arrived weren't important. It was just an attempt to buy them more time.

At sunset, I saw Amer waving to us from behind the fence. I walked over to hear what he was saying.

"I told the police about you, and they told me to call you, but you need to come from the back door."

We didn't waste a second. We walked surreptitiously to where Amer guided us to go and saw him with Linda and an officer.

"Who are these?" asked the officer, like Amer hadn't mentioned us.

"These are my wife and my other toddler, and the rest are my brothers."

"You said your family was waiting outside, not your brothers. Now get out of here you all!" raged the officer.

7
The Gate of Hell
"Get the hell in!"

"Amer, calm down a bit … Talk to me," Haya said as she jogged to catch up to him.

"They want us to get in through the gate. We will get in as they wish." He wasn't listening to anyone.

Amer was snappish, and we knew he had lost his temper. He reached the crowd and shouted while jostling against the people, "Get out of my way! Now! You all saw that I was in there for six hours!"

Normally, people didn't like his attitude and argued with him, but he was so furious that people decided to let him do whatever he wanted. After unwillingly fighting with people, we stood close to the gate.

A lady from inside the police station drew people's attention while yelling over a loudspeaker in Arabic, "If you don't organize yourself, I will call the police to send you back to your countries!"

Her words made the crowd acrimonious; it was like pouring water on burning oil, and everyone tried to open the gate with their bare hands. Threatening the people to send them back to their countries wasn't the best thing to say after six hours waiting on a scorching day.

We were jam-packed, surrounded by throngs of people who were trying to get as close as possible to the gate. People were constantly pushing each other. Three hours passed, and the conditions only got worse because more people were coming from the second camp. We wanted to get out of the unbearable crowdedness, but it was hopeless. Hundreds of people were stacked behind us.

Both Abdo and Linda had had enough. We, the adults couldn't stand it anymore, and the toddlers had every right to cry out loud. I carried Abdo on my head so that he could breathe, and Othman did the same with Linda.

I was crammed in with more bodies than I could

The crowd gathering closer to the gate

count even in a photograph, and I was unable to avoid the coughs and sneezes of strangers. I could smell them, too. There was an unholy agglomeration of body odour, and my cologne wasn't any better.

All of a sudden, Ghaithaa fainted. Mohammad got down to sprinkle water on her face to help her regain consciousness—and then he suffocated and fainted as well. We shouted at people that we had an emergency and to give us some space to get out of the crowd. The volunteers heard us and rushed for help. We all could get out, but Amer stayed near the gate. Mohamad and Ghaithaa were laid on the ground away from the crowd.

A police officer showed up from behind the fence with Salam, the guy who had offered to drive us to the second camp. He said that only five families would get in, and he had papers with numbers from one to five. Salam remembered Amer and gave him number five. We had to fight our way back in so we could enter when the gate opened. I carried Abdo again on my head. We waited for half an hour.

"They won't open it," said Mohamad. "They are just saying that to control the people. Let's get out of here—even if we have to sleep in the street."

I told Othman and Haya that we were getting out. We had been like this for more than nine hours, and we could no longer stand it. On our way out to painful freedom, in the middle of the people, the gate opened!

Not only the fence gate opened; the gate which held the adrenaline in my veins opened as well. Everyone charged towards the gate. Abdo pulled my hair firmly with his tiny fingers and shouted a terrifying cry, declaring war. We were pushing out, and people were pushing in. The people flowed like rivers, never stopping for obstacles but swirling around them. We had to go with the current.

Amer carried Linda and ran to the gate. Othman grabbed Haya's hand and went after Amer. The police officers were closing the gate to keep people from getting in, and Ghaithaa got stuck between the people—but Mohamad forced and pushed her in. He tried to follow her, but he saw a woman holding a baby and looking terrified, not knowing what to do or where to go. He held the gate with his hands to keep it open, and at least twenty people were pushing him from behind.

"Get the hell in! What are you waiting for!" he seethed.

The woman got in with her baby, and Mohamad made it as well. I heard Othman shouting, "Hand me Abdo! Give him to me!"

I lifted Abdo and tried to hand him to Othman. My brother could catch the boy's hand and grab him. Now I was the only one left.

I tried to get in, but I was jostled in all directions by people. My hair was pulled, my jacket got torn in the underarm, my feet were stepped on, and before I was trampled underfoot, I was cruelly pushed to the fence and my lips kissed it. I grasped the gate with my hand, but halfway there, the gate closed on my body. My body got crushed; half of it was inside and the other half was outside. My leg got stuck, and my back was getting smashed slowly but strongly.

Mohamad positioned his foot on the fence and grabbed me forcefully in. I made it and rolled on the ground. I was the last person to get in.

I lay on the ground. I stood up, walked two steps, and crumpled to my knees. I was just shouting, "Oh my God!" My hands wouldn't stop shaking. My legs couldn't carry me, and my lungs ran out of air. I didn't know whether to breathe, to walk, or to stay still. I was just focusing on consuming as much oxygen as possible.

Haya was holding both Abdo and Linda, who were howling. They were horrified. They had never experienced such a clash before, and they should never have. Ghaithaa's whole body was trembling; she was fatigued. Mohamad held her hand and tried to calm her down.

"If I knew we were going to face this, I would never have thought of taking you with me," he said. "I swear there won't be any difficulties from now on. It will be OK."

He looked at me and Othman and gestured for us to talk to her.

Man, I am trying to breathe over here.

Amer was trying to keep himself cool and to cool Haya down. Othman carried Abdo and walked him around.

The people who got in were all nervous and tired. The voices of crying kids and women were all around us. Those who couldn't make it were trying desperately to get in and convince the police officer to open the gate. He refused.

The police station was divided into two sections separated by a fence. We sat under a high lamp post, as night had fallen. Abdo finally fell asleep in Othman's arms, but he wasn't breathing normally. He was inhaling heavily every couple of seconds. It took us some time to wind down a little.

"Man, our teamwork was lit!" Othman prattled.

"Mohamad was funny," I giggled. "He pushing that, bulling that, and running people over."

"Did you see that woman? God, she was killing me!"

"You can't blame her. Everyone was stressed out," said Ghaithaa.

"I can't believe this is happening to us," sighed Haya.

"Dear Abdo and Linda. I feel sorry for them," added Amer.

We were glad to be on the other side of the gate, even if we had to sleep on the bare ground. Laith's family wasn't around. Maybe they got their white cards and were on their way to Athens.

Everyone saw the one guy who climbed the fence and jumped to the other side. Unfortunately, a police officer noticed him from a distance. He walked to the guy with rage radiating from his narrowed rigid eyes. Angry eyes were just the start; then came the slamming and the clipped swears. He punched the guy straight in the stomach, kicked him back over the fence, and continued beating him recklessly, like a punching bag.

People rushed to help the guy and keep the police officer from causing serious damage. The officer pulled the guy by his hair to the back door and shoved him through. The Red Cross volunteers were angry with the police officer. He swore at them, slammed the door, and walked back to his office.

Sadly, there was nothing to do. Calling the police would have been a good idea, but we were inside the police station, and it was a police officer who assaulted the victim.

After one hour, two lines for families and non-families were formed. We stood in line for about half an hour, but the line didn't seem to be moving smoothly. Haya went to see what was the issue. She talked with a police officer, and he told her to bring our passports and come back to him. We followed her and showed him our passports, and he let us in. We learned our lesson: always find a way to get in, otherwise, you will stay out.

There were six offices with five police officers each. Most of them were just sitting in the offices doing nothing but drinking tea. All the chaos outside the gate could have been prevented by at least three police officers, but they didn't bother themselves.

While we were waiting for our turn to get the white card, we saw Salam.

"I wish we had agreed to you driving us before," said Amer with regret.

"It is OK," Salam replied.

"What do we do next after we get our white cards?"

"After you get your white cards, you need to take a ferry to Athens, and then you will continue to Macedonia. If you like, I can drive you there, but you need to wait a bit. There is a family that I am going to drive there first."

We told him that we could wait, and he gave us his phone number. People who got their white card were being sent out of the police station, to be replaced by those who were waiting outside.

In the police office, we got photographed and waited for the officers to finish typing on their keyboards and sign a piece of paper that looked like a cipher with the Greek letters and symbols. And that was it. Totally worth the fight.

After we got our white cards, we sat outside the police station happily waiting for Salam. People were heading to the highway in a group, and they told us there was a bus we could take to the port for free. Before we followed them, Amer called Salam to make sure it was OK to take the bus. Salam gave us his approval.

We arrived at the port at 01:35. The ferry was scheduled to depart at 03:00. We were asked to show our white cards at the ticket office. A ticket for adults coasted 51 euros. Toddlers were free of charge.

The ferry was gigantic—about ten thousand tonnes of ancient rusting metal, carrying hundreds of cars that were but toys compared to it. A noisy vibrating engine rattled the earth. Lifeboats hung on rusted chains off the weather-worn deck. Yes, it was my first time riding this monster. I found it kind of funny to pay 1,000 USD for a rubber boat and 72 euros for a ferry.

The inside wasn't as fascinating as the outside. Human bodies were all over the floor. It felt like walking into a crime scene. There was barely space to walk. Sleeping on the floor to save money was what we planned to do, but after searching for an empty spot for half an hour, we surrendered and decided to book a room.

Haya and I went to the reception desk to check the price for one night, and it was 83 euros per room. We couldn't book one room only; we were informed that a room could have up to four people, no more, so we had to book two rooms. We took the keys and turned around to find a guy wearing turquoise shorts and a straw hat and holding black sunglasses. But it was obvious that he was a refugee, like us.

"Hello, friend! Do you speak English?" he asked in an Iraqi accent.

"Yes, I do. How can I help you?"

"Good. Can you ask the receptionist if they have Kofe?"

"Sorry, I don't understand. What is *Kofe*?" I thought it was an Iraqi word that I didn't know.

"Uhm, it is Kofe, in Syria. You say Kahwa maybe." He was spelling *coffee* in an Arabic accent for some reason. Haya was holding back her laughter. I asked the receptionist, and she showed us where to get coffee.

"Can you ask her one more thing? Can you ask if they have room service for breakfast?"

I couldn't help but smile at him. Sadly for him, they didn't have room service.

"OK, my friend, thanks a lot for your help!" said the man.

"You are welcome!"

He had all the right to ask for coffee and room service; I just found it kind of funny that in spite of just surviving death, some people can still enjoy life no matter what.

Othman, Mohamad, Amer, and I were in one room, with Haya, Ghaithaa, and the toddlers in the room next to ours. The room had two bunk beds and a toilet with a shower—all we ever needed.

After Othman took a shower, it was my turn. I got out of the shower, and he was snoring a symphony on the bottom mattress. I climbed the two steps to my salvation and was asleep within seconds.

Wednesday/14-10-2015/11:50

Eight hours of deep sleep were a treatment to my body. However, the waking-up part was the worst. Dizziness was all I felt. My head was throbbing, and I didn't know if my arm was numb or broken. It took me quite a bit of time before I got out of bed and stretched my body.

Amer's phone was ringing.

"Who is it?" Mohamad asked.

"I don't know the number," Amer shrugged. He picked up the phone and said, "Hello?"

"Amer!"

"Ezz!"

"Is it Ezz?!" I flew to Amer.

"Yes!" Amer put him on speaker. "Where have you been?! I called you many times, but you didn't answer."

"Water got into my phone, and it stopped working," Ezz replied. "I am calling from a guy's phone that I met in Greece. Is everyone OK?"

"Yeah, don't worry. Where are you now?" asked Amer.

"I am about to leave Athens. I wanted to wait for you, but I didn't know your location, plus I don't have any place to stay."

"Is it true that they were sending people back from Izmir?" Amer asked.

"Don't name that ominous city," replied Ezz. "The police chased us, and we had to hide in a mountain until they were gone. The bloody trafficker forced us to take the rubber boat in the middle of the night. How did I survive? I have no fricking idea."

"What is important is that you are in Greece now," Amer reassured him.

"Yeah. Amer, I need to hang up and call your parents. They must be worried."

I sank into the mattress. Finally, Ezz had called us. A mountain of burden was lifted from my shoulders when I heard Ezz's voice. The thought of never seeing him again vanished. And now was the time to enjoy breakfast. We hadn't had food for almost a whole day. Ghaithaa, Haya, and the toddlers were awake as well, and we all went to the buffet, where toast with butter and jam were served.

"Yazan? Hi!" I saw him filling his plate.

"Oh, hello, guys! Glad to see you again!" He came over to us.

"Where have you been?" I asked.

"I think I was sent to a different camp. I had to wait for two days to get my white card."

As we chatted, we found out that there were other police stations from where refugees got their white cards.

With two hours left, we roamed around the deck, not minding the wind that tousled and blew my hair. We were embraced by the blue. I wasn't sure if the sky reflected its colour or the sea did. They were identical twins: one with soaring white seagulls and one with leaping grey dolphins.

Me holding Abdo holding a banana

With the high sound of the horn, our trip on the ferry came to an end. The hallways were cramped with people, and we waited until most people left. Some people welcomed us with signs saying, "Welcome to Athens!" which warmed our hearts, while others welcomed us with signs saying, "Need a bus?"

As Yazan had said, we needed to take a bus from Athens to the Macedonian border. We were the last to get off the ferry, and all the buses going to the Macedonian border were full. We had to wait for buses to come.

"Hello! Please take these for your babies." An old Greek lady gave us diapers and biscuits for Abdo and Linda. There was affection in her smile—a gentleness that seemed so innocent and genuine and could only be found in someone who is truly kind.

A bus arrived after some minutes. We got on, but we were around twelve people only. We expected the bus to drive us to the Macedonian border directly. Instead, we drove to a bus office just a couple of kilometres away.

"A bus is coming to drive you to the Macedonian border" was what the owner of the office told us.

The price of the tickets was 15 euros for adults. After we paid, Amer disappeared for some time. When he came back, I asked him where he was.

"I was just checking something," he told me. I knew he was trying to hide something, but I just let go.

We waited for one hour, but no bus appeared. We asked the owner if there was a problem, and he answered, "I ordered a double-decker bus instead of two separate buses. It will arrive soon."

More people were coming to the office and buying tickets. We waited for another hour, but the bus still didn't show up. We suspected that we had been scammed. We talked to the owner again and asked for clarification.

"The bus had to wait on the way here. One more hour and it will be here. However, it is better for you. You will arrive in Macedonia at dawn, and there won't be many people there."

The answer wasn't convincing. We knew that he only wanted to save diesel and get more people on the bus. People weren't happy and argued with the owner, but he kept saying that the bus was on the way. There was nothing else to do but discover the town.

The office was in a crowded, small maze of narrow streets leading to an ancient church. Mixed smells and flavours were floating in the air, coming from the fast-food trucks on every corner. After five hours, and while we were eating croissants, the imaginary double-decker bus finally came true.

8
Endless Rain
"They are slaughtering people!"

Thursday/15-10-2015/06:19

When we arrived at the Macedonian border, everything was grey. A vast blanket of grey sat heavily upon the earth. Dense fog with tiny drops of water swooped in and skirted around the trees like a giant eraser.

We weren't the only ones to arrive. We had company: six other buses drove to Macedonia at dawn too. The Macedonian border patrol gave each bus a piece of paper with a number. Ours was 5, and it was given to a guy on our bus.

We got off the bus as one group. We hardly noticed the large tent at the border—like the first tent in Greece only worse. Its condition was so atrocious that people preferred to wait outside in the freezing cold.

The border patrol didn't tell us how long we were going to wait, but they were letting the groups go in order. A long time after, when we were about to turn into ice statues, an officer yelled, "All right, group number 5, gather yourself!"

We formed a group and walked to the border patrol.

"Show me the number," said the officer.

We waited for the guy who had the number. He didn't show up. Everyone searched for him, but he couldn't be found anywhere. He had most likely sneaked into another group and got away. We didn't think it would be the end of the world.

"If you don't have a number, you won't pass," yelled the officer.

We explained that the person ran away and that was why we didn't have a number, but he was determined, and he didn't care about the shivering kids.

Come on. Are we not going to pass for just a little piece of paper?

Othman and I complained to another patrol about the stupidity of waiting half an hour for a lost paper. He talked to his stone-headed comrade and convinced the man that we weren't playing rock-paper-scissors. In this case, there wasn't a need for a paper to beat a stone. Finally, the officer agreed to let us through. He was just having some fun making our journey harder.

We were told to follow the train rail. We did as we were told, and after fifteen minutes of walking, we found a gathering of hundreds of people on the barren and empty ground next to a large black shelter. These were the groups who preceded us. It was obvious that we were going to wait for hours. And we did.

"Please stick to your group and stand in lines. We will take each group to the shelter to proceed with the white card."

Yes. There was a Macedonian white card as well.

Each hour, a group of people was sent to the shelter to proceed with their white cards. Meanwhile, there was an American volunteer who laughed and played with the kids. He carried Abdo on his head and ran while screaming: "Here comes John Cena!" The other kids were running after him with joy.

When it was finally our group's turn, we entered the shelter. It was full of wooden benches. We gave our white cards to the police along with our passports and identity cards. We were given drawstring bags which had written on them

Donation from the KSA. Each contained a banana, a chocolate croissant, a piece of bread, a single-serving packet of jam, orange juice, and a bottle of water.

While we were eating, two guys and a girl wearing clown outfits with large hands and feet jumped on the tables. They blew the kids' minds when they made a tissue vanish and grabbed a coin from their ears.

How awesome are these people? I thought. *They left their homes and came here just to entertain the kids and play with them. They chose to spend their job holidays with these kids instead of being in a five-star hotel. What wonderful hearts they must have.*

The police started shouting out the names of people whose white cards were finished. They shouted our names as well and gave us back our documents and the white cards.

It was sprinkling when we left the shelter. The volunteers were giving people plastic raincoats, but they had only one left to give to us, along with a small umbrella. Othman carried Linda after he dressed her in the raincoat, and Amer held the umbrella for Abdo while carrying him.

We were on our own from now on. They said we could take a bus or a taxi to Serbia. It was up to us.

On the way out of the shelter, the American volunteer approached me and asked, "How do you feel, young man?"

"A bit tired, but I can manage myself. Thanks for asking."

"That is the spirit," said the volunteer, putting a hand on my shoulder. "You have a long journey ahead of you, but I am more than confident that you can do it. Stay strong!"

"I will. Thanks a lot for your support!" I wouldn't call this a meaningless conversation. In fact, I felt much more confident that I could face the whole world. That man came the whole way from America to tell me these words—words I would never forget.

We walked with a group of people until we crossed a little bridge where buses and taxis were waiting for us. The buses were full in an instant, so taxis were our only option. Two taxi drivers offered to drive us; one taxi couldn't fit us all.

"OK," Amer agreed, "but under one condition. Both taxis must drive together. We don't want to get separated."

The taxi drivers were relatives, so they had no problem with that.

Othman, Yazan, and I got in one taxi, and the rest of us got in the second taxi. It cost us 20 euros each. I sat in the back seat looking through a window at the green rug of trees that covered the mountains and the fog that hid the peaks, not to forget the running rivers making their way forcibly between the solid harsh mountains. I never knew Macedonia was that beautiful. I never knew it was going to heal my soul.

"Mohi, wake up! We arrived." Othman nudged me.

We had been driving for three hours. I opened my eyes slightly and looked through the window to see nothing but a poor land. We got out of the taxi, gathered our bags, and stood in front of an open rusty iron gate. We were the only ones there. Taxis are faster than buses, so the others were yet to arrive.

"You will continue walking from here to Serbia," the driver told us. "The taxi cannot go farther."

We walked through the gate and followed the train rail along with Yazan. It didn't seem to have an end, but once it made a turn to the right, we took off in another direction towards the cracked paved road, as the taxi driver had told us.

There was a narrow stream that we had to cross. Fortunately, a tree trunk had been made into a bridge, probably by the previous refugees on their way to Serbia. Yazan crossed the trunk first, swiftly. Amer followed him with Abdo. Halfway across, Yazan took Abdo from him. Mohamad handed Linda to Amer, who crossed the trunk with her. Haya and Othman made it safely too.

With her second step on the trunk, Ghaithaa's foot slipped, and half of her body fell into the stream. She would have fallen completely if Mohamad hadn't caught her. Still, she sprained her ankle.

I crossed the trunk with no problem, but my shoes got covered in wet mud.

We took a little rest under a tree to check Ghaihtaa's injury; which was thankfully not serious, and rest a bit before we continued walking. We thought that it was going to take one or two hours to get to Serbia. Little did we know.

The rain wasn't slowing down. We had to move faster before it got worse. I got tired of holding Abdo. Yazan was nice and offered to carry him on his head. Othman carried Linda instead of Amer. We reached an army checkpoint and were concerned. However, they acted normally and let us pass through the checkpoint without intervention.

An hour after passing the checkpoint, we were nowhere. Yazan had helped us a lot, but we couldn't let him carry Abdo all the way.

"I appreciate your help, Yazan, but it is OK. We can carry Abdo," said Amer.

"No, no need to say that," he replied.

"Thank you. Still, you don't have to. We are a family, and we will only hold you up."

"OK," said Yazan finally. "I will try to see if I can get some help and get back to you. See you in Serbia!"

He handed Abdo to me and slowly faded away. Minutes later, a pickup came towards us and slowed down until it stopped by us.

"Hello, guys! Need raincoats?" a man asked us in an American accent.

"Yes, please!" we answered.

He got out of his pickup, opened the trunk, and gave each of us a blue plastic raincoat. We wore them on top of our backpacks so they kept more water from getting into them and ruining the food. He apologized that he couldn't offer more help and drive us to Serbia, but that would be considered human trafficking and would get him into trouble.

"Can I ask you guys—why did you leave Syria? I do want to hear the stories of refugees."

"I don't know where to start," said Othman. "There wasn't one reason; there were plenty. I got arrested on the way back home from high school because a demonstration was held at my school. Both my parents were terrified that I would get arrested again."

Mohamad added, "I also got arrested and was tortured for a whole day due to the similarity of names. I mean, my name is Mohamad. I was definitely going to encounter the same issue again."

"I didn't leave Syria with my family," said Amer. "I had a good job, and my wife and I used to sleep in the store or at her relatives' place after I lost my apartment. One day, my wife was feeling sick, so we went to the doctor and were shocked to learn that she was pregnant with triplets after five years of marriage! I was OK risking my life as long as I could afford to live, but when I knew I was going to be a father of three children, I didn't want them to be born in war. I had no choice but to move to my family in Turkey. Unfortunately, one of the babies couldn't make it to life, and we only have twins now."

"Wow! Triplets at once," said the volunteer. "As a father myself, let me tell you, you did the right thing. Their future is in your hands." He turned to me. "And what about you? What is your name?"

"Mohi." I was still struggling to put the raincoat on.

"You look the youngest. Why did you leave Syria?"

The reason I left? I didn't leave Syria on my own; I just followed my parents as my brothers and sister did. But I remembered the night that we didn't want to risk our lives after.

"As my brother said," I began, "there were many reasons, but I remember when my parents chose to leave our homeland. We lived in Jobar, a town in Damascus. On the first day of Ramadan 2012, the month that Muslims fast from the sunrise to the sunset, we were having Suhur at 02:00; a light meal before the sunrise, and getting ready for the first day of Ramadan when our landline phone rang. It was my cousin. He said, 'Clear the apartment immediately and head to the cellar! The army is on its way, and they are slaughtering people!'"

The expression on the American man's face implied his interest, so I continued.

"We noticed how my father's face changed after the call ended. He looked at us in the eye, and we knew something terrible was about to happen. He said, 'We are going to the cellar. Move!' We left the food on the table, locked the door, and got out of the apartment. Within five minutes, the whole neighbourhood gathered in the street in the darkest of the night. It was true; everyone had been told the same thing. The army was coming to annihilate us.

"My aunt's building had a large cellar where all the women, children, and elders could hide. My cousin was standing next to me talking to his panicking sister, who lived ten minutes away from us. 'They killed two men and arrested seven,' she said. 'The women in the building next to us are being raped! I am so scared! I don't know what to do! Please pray for me and take care of your parents!'

"Thank God we were armed. We were holding broomsticks to defend our families. Broomsticks versus real heavy weapons. We had no chance against them. We heard the cry, 'They arrived! The army arrived! Run!' Staying meant waiting for our death. Everyone called their families and ran away. I, my family, and my old grandmother started running in terror through the narrow streets to nowhere. Seconds later, we heard shooting and screaming. We felt death upon us, and we accepted it."

"Please tell me you all survived!" said the man anxiously.

"Well, I am standing here. We were the luckiest people to escape. Sadly, many others weren't lucky. We walked through fields avoiding the army all night until we reached our relatives who lived in a town near us. We stayed at their place for four days. It wasn't safe yet to go back to our apartment. The army was arresting everyone from my town.

"The next day, my father came home and said, 'We are traveling to Egypt next week. I have already booked the tickets.' He had had enough. He didn't want to risk the lives of his family anymore, and before waiting to lose a family member, my father had resolved to flee Syria.

"I cried and shouted at him. I called him a coward like everyone did. I was just a 14-year-old boy who wanted to spend his day out playing football and video games with his friends, but my father didn't want to see fear in his kids' eyes ever again. In Syria, we weren't living; we were only surviving."

"This is unbelievable," said the volunteer. "Why would someone your age experience such tragedy?" His grip hardened on the door of the pickup, his white face turned red, he ground his teeth, and his eyes looked sorry for me and enraged at the world. He wanted to know why the world was like this. Why were people getting killed? Why were people watching but not acting? Why did injustice exist? He had countless questions, but I didn't know the answers. He was speechless.

"I don't honestly know what to say," he admitted. "I feel like I've lost hope in this hellish world, but then I see you fighting for a better life. I am sorry I can't do much to help. Take good care of yourselves, and good luck for the rest of your journey!"

Our first-floor apartment in Jobar

He got in his pickup and drove away, maybe to hear more stories. Ours wasn't the only one.

After living in the past, I came back to the draining present. We trudged for two hours and saw nothing but empty arid fields topped by a mysterious mist. We were terribly exhausted. We weren't athletes, and I am pretty sure even athletes would have had a bad time walking in such conditions.

Othman and I were taking turns carrying Abdo. We made sure that the toddlers were wrapped wholly in their clothes so they didn't get sick, but we knew that they were definitely going to feel ill. They should have been in their cosy warm beds sleeping peacefully with their bellies full, not here, in a place that was harsh for grown-ups.

"Let's take a little break," Mohamad said. "Ghaithaa can't walk on her ankle."

Yes! Please! We just instantly sat on the wet harsh ground.

"Is Abdo cold, Mohi?" Haya asked wearily.

"A little bit. He is asleep."

"Ugh," she said. "Who knew that we would end up here?"

Even though we were starving for some rest, we had to keep moving. The gentle rain was turning into heavy water balloons.

Long afterwards, we started seeing a few people walking ahead of us. They were also refugees, probably the ones who arrived in Macedonia before we did. We saw an old mother carrying two backpacks and her little daughter on her back. She was plodding two steps and stopping to take a break, again and again. She was snivelling in silence—not because she was ashamed but because she had run out of tears, the only thing that could help her.

She got up again to walk and stopped again. I wanted to help the old lady like I used to do when I was a child, like my parents taught me. There was no "but" and no excuse. There was an old drained lady and an exhausted me carrying a cold toddler on my chest and a heavy wet bag on my back.

I was no longer a human. All I wanted was to relax. My body screamed in soreness. I didn't know how to feel—to feel sorry for her, to feel contempt for my weakness, to hate myself, or to console myself that there was nothing I could do. All I knew was that it really hurt, so badly. And I did nothing.

We had passed the old struggling mother an hour ago. She was left behind all alone. After all that time, I was done. My feelings evaporated. I felt nothing.

My aching body wasn't annoying me anymore. I was in total surrender, a body without a soul, just like zombies tottering and swaying from side to side. Nobody spoke a word. The sound of the heavy rain hitting the plastic raincoat and my heavy breath, followed by a cloud of water vapor, were the only things that could be heard. The feeling that I could face the whole world vanished. The world was harsh and I was but a feeble, helpless person.

I remembered when my mother used to scold me whenever I refused to wear heavy clothes and a beanie when it was cold and smiled ironically. *What would my mother say if she saw me walking in the rain not wearing heavy clothes? Would she scold me again?*

"I ... I see a village."

Othman's words brought me back to life. Finally! A village! We were thrilled but weren't able to celebrate and walk any faster.

We got closer and saw houses. The lights were turned on but the curtains were closed. People were knocking on the doors asking for water but were ignored. No one offered help; they chose to pretend we didn't exist.

I asked a guy what to do next, but he had no idea, just like us. Later, a guy who didn't seem to be a refugee came to me and said, "*Assalamu alaikum*! Are you looking for someone to drive you? My father and I have taxis."

Did he just say "assalamu alaikum"? That was unexpected. We asked him where we should go, and he told us that we needed to apply for a white card—again, just when I thought there wouldn't be more difficulties. The police station was a hundred kilometres away. Of course, no more walking.

"Here, let me carry the toddler for you, and you can follow me!" the driver said, carrying Abdo. We followed him for ten long minutes in the village, and then he shouted in Serbian to someone standing near a taxi. It was his father. He jogged towards us with a smile on his face.

"*Assalamu alaikum*! Don't worry, you are our brothers and sisters. Please let me help you carry your bags!" I felt reassured. In the past days, only a few people had smiled at us.

Amer, Haya, and the toddlers got into the father's taxi, while Othman, Mohamad, Ghaithaa, and I got into the son's. The moment I plopped heavily into the seat, I felt my legs burning and shaking, I expected to relax, but instead, pain started to penetrate my body. I almost cried.

"It is cold out there," said the son. "I will turn on the heat."

Night had already fallen. I was looking through the window. Everything seemed gloomy: the rain, the fog, and the half-destroyed buildings. It felt like a war zone. I was surprised once again when I heard the Azan, the Islamic call to prayer.

The son explained that there were Muslims in Serbia and that those buildings had been damaged during the Second World War. The government was too poor to rebuild them.

He continued talking about the history of his country until we reached a police checkpoint. The father's taxi stopped at the checkpoint for a minute and then got through.

We stopped at the checkpoint, and the police officer got close to the driver's window and started talking in Serbian with the son. They talked for about five minutes and were pointing at us. We had no clue what was going on. The son got out of the taxi and continued talking with the police officer. After a while, he got in the taxi again and told us that it was OK. The police officer needed a bribe.

We got through the checkpoint and found the father's taxi waiting for us to drive together.

"How much is the cost?" asked Mohamad.

"Only five euros. The cost of the diesel. If you don't have money, it is completely OK."

"It is OK, we can pay," said Mohamad. "Thanks for your kindness."

They weren't joking when they called us brothers and sisters.

It was still raining when we stood in a line to enter the police station. The line looked unending. We could only see a shelter where people probably applied for the white card. The cold reached into our bones, and standing still made our bodies even colder, as the energy which we didn't have in the first place was being consumed.

Haya was rubbing Linda's cold tiny body to warm her, but her crying kept getting louder. She was coughing as if she was a smoker and ended up throwing up. Amer took Linda and walked away from the crowd to try to put her to sleep.

After what seemed like a decade, the line started moving slowly. We took our first step, but Amer was nowhere to be found. I searched around for him, but it seemed to be in vain.

Then, suddenly, I heard, "Mohi!" Amer was waving at me.

"Where were you, man?! Don't just disappe—"

"I got the white card," he said.

"Wait, really?"

"Yes," he assured me. "Tell your brothers to come here now!"

My brothers followed me hesitantly. We met Amer in a small shelter where an old man was standing next to him. It was this man who had helped Amer get his white card. He told us not to draw attention and stay quiet.

"Only one person follow me. The rest wait outside," he said in broken Arabic. His origin was Arab, but he had been living in Serbia for over forty-six years.

Five minutes later, Mohamad came out with our white cards. We could barely contain ourselves from jumping for joy and exposing him. Looking at the never-ending line, we knew we would have waited at least eight hours in the rain if it wasn't for that old man.

"Where should we go now?" Amer asked.

"You see the buses waiting outside the fence? They are waiting to be full to go. They will drive you to Hungary. But take that brown bus. It is for Syrians."

We thanked him again. The second we passed the fence, the bus drivers went crazy over us and grabbed us by our clothes to get on their buses. We felt like celebrities. Still, we ignored them and headed to the brown bus.

We were about to get on when the driver said, "You can't get on. You are too many."

"We are only six people and two toddlers that we can hold in our lap," replied Mohamad.

"Let them get on. There are empty places in the back," a guy said from the back of the bus.

"Whatever. Get on and manage yourself," said the driver.

We sat in the back seats, and we were the last ones on. The bus wasn't any better than the one we took in Turkey; in fact, it was even smaller. It was dilapidated, yet riding it was a hundred times better than walking.

"Hello again!" said a familiar voice. It was Yazan.

"I knew we could not lose you," chirped Othman.

"How did you get your white cards this fast? I arrived first and had to wait for two hours."

"You can say it is a miracle," Amer replied.

"Well, I'm glad we are together again."

"Have you guys met before?" interrupted the guy who told the driver to let us get on.

"Yes, we met on the Turkish island, got separated twice, and met again," Amer answered.

"It is good to have company on this journey. My name is Sleman, and this is my wife, Diyala."

We chatted a bit and got to know them. They were so sweet. They were Kurdish and lived in northern Syria. Sleman had bronzed skin with dimples that showed up whenever he smiled, honest brown eyes, and a buzz-cut hairstyle. His wife, Diyala, shared the same skin tone but with darker brown eyes and longer black hair.

"Aren't you hungry?" I asked Othman.

He didn't answer. I looked at him and saw that he had leant against the window and was already asleep. I grabbed the piece of bread with the packet of jam and the orange juice and ate while enjoying the view through the raindrops on the window.

9
A Wild Chase
"I said stop!"

Friday/16-10-2015/08:40

"Morning, y'all. You arrived," said the driver sarcastically.

I held my hand in front of my eyes to block the light. It wasn't like I was sleeping; I had barely been able to sleep for two hours, being awakened several times by the unsteady movement of the bus. I looked through the window to see that we were surrounded by cornfields in every direction.

"What do you mean, 'you arrived'?" a guy asked.

"If you want, I can drive you some more kilometres, but you need to pay five extra euros each," answered the driver with a sly smile on his face.

"We have already paid ten euros!" protested Yazan.

"You pay or you get off. I don't have time to waste," the driver snapped.

Everyone on the bus was triggered by the way we were patronized and refused to pay, which provoked the driver in return and made him shout, "OK, leave the bus. You don't deserve my offer. Now get lost in these cornfields! Make sure to walk in groups; gangsters might attack and rob you," he yelled as we got off the bus. As if *he* didn't try to rob us.

I had known that we might have to walk to the Hungarian border, but I didn't think about walking through towering cornfields. I carried Linda and prepared myself for hours of hiking.

"You know what, Amer, I heard that the Hungarian army is not so friendly," said Sleman, worried. "They are attacking and hitting refugees and not allowing them to enter Hungary."

"Honestly, I've started to regret my decision to go on this journey," replied Amer. "I mean, I can handle it, but my toddlers … Look at Abdo, awake in the middle of nowhere, not knowing what is going on."

"Oh, look at you, little hero," Sleman said, tickling Abdo. "You are a strong man, and when you grow up, your father will tell you about your big adventure."

Abdo laughed in the way only a baby can laugh: a sweet sound unblemished by the hurts of life.

"*InshaAllah*, their future will be better than ours," Amer said as he kissed Abdo's head.

We were about forty persons, and we moved in a big group, but unfortunately, all the phones were out of battery. Only one guy had his phone working, and even then, there was no network coverage. So we decided to follow the path of the bus. There were five single guys, including Yazan, moving freely. The rest were families, with four kids between the age of 5 and 12 years.

A really old woman with the face of someone who has lived, suffered, loved, and grieved—which made her look around 85 years old—was wearing a violet hijab that covered her upper body and a black skirt tucked into green socks. She had a hunchback and clearly had knee problems; it took effort for her to walk steadily. She had one foot in the grave. She had lived in her country for decades but now was forced to leave it to live. It is the human instinct to survive that drove her to leave everything she had, like everyone else.

At that age, she wasn't searching for a better life to build her future in a foreign country with a language she didn't speak and traditions she wasn't used to. She was already in her future. All she wanted to do at that age was wake up in the morning in her old yet tidy house to the music of dozens of birds, water the plants on her window that were probably older than me, make black coffee, and wait for her lovely neighbour who she used to play with as a kid to gossip about her unlovely neighbour who didn't yet return the Tefal pot she'd borrowed.

Her son, a man in his forties, was the only one she had left. He was by her side, helping her keep up with the group.

I shouldn't be complaining, right? I thought as I looked at her.

A razor fence appeared in the distance. It didn't seem to have a gate or a place to enter through, but a green army jeep with giant wheels sat on the other side of it. Beside the jeep stood three soldiers in green and brown camouflage baggy uniforms and matching caps. Their trousers were tucked into light brown combat boots.

We approached the razor fence, and Yazan walked close to the soldiers.

"Hello!" he said. "How can we come in?"

"What? I can't hear you. Come closer!" said the soldier. Something in his tone felt suspicious.

"How can we come in?" repeated Yazan after getting closer.

The soldier then sprayed Yazan and the rest of the group with tear gas. In a moment, the screams of the group were heard loudly, and everything turned into chaos. We were in the back of the group, and those who were in the front ran towards us shouting, "Get out! Cover your eyes!"

I put my palm over Linda's whole face while holding her with the other hand like a bag of potatoes and ran away along with my brothers.

"You son of a... Why would you ... Damn!" swore a guy while he was coughing.

"Go back to your country!" a soldier fired back as he watched us from behind the razor fence.

"You low-life cowards! Why would you do that!" the guy shouted again.

"Go back to your country!" shouted the soldier back and stood there watching us from behind the fence.

Although I had not been near the fence, the gas spread quickly, and I couldn't cover my eyes because I was holding Linda. My eyes filled with tears and were badly irritated. My face itched, and I painfully coughed sputum.

Luckily, a guy had a medium bottle of Coke and rushed to pour some on my and others' faces. I handed Linda to Othman and fought to stop myself from rubbing my eyes, because it would only increase the intensity of the pain.

"Let's move back a little. They might do something crazy again!" said Sleman loudly so everyone could hear him. We did as he suggested.

"Are you better now?" Mohamad asked, approaching Yazan.

"Those bitc … the gas entered my lungs," replied Yazan, holding his eyes wide open.

We decided to sit between the cornfields to hide and rest a bit. But hundreds of bugs climbing our bodies didn't make the place any too comfortable.

The sun had risen completely. Our sight got better and our bodies got some rest. We had been keeping an eye out for soldiers, but none seemed to be around. We weren't sure that we were on the right track, but we continued following the path of the bus through the cornfields from a distance. Thankfully, Ghaithaa's ankle was a bit better, and she was able to walk instead of limp.

The young guys suggested that they walk in front to warn the group if they saw any soldiers. The families walked behind.

"Stop moving!" a guy warned us at one point. "Two men are approaching us. They are not soldiers, but stay still for a moment."

We saw Yazan and the other guys talking with the men. One of them was tall and had a moustache; the other was shorter and bald. They were Hungarian. The guys then led them to us.

"Who are these men?" Mohamad asked.

"They say that they are smugglers and have taxis to drive us to Hungary," Yazan answered.

"Hello!" said the tall guy. "We can give you a ride to Budapest, where you can take the train. We are here to help you." He seemed to have done this hundreds of times before.

"Yes," added the short guy. "You are a large group. If you get caught, the army will force you to give your fingerprint and stay in Hungary. You don't need that to happen to you."

"Let's say we agree," a man from our group asked. "Do you have enough taxis? And how much do you need?"

"Sure, our friends have taxis that are waiting for you. We usually take more, but since Hungary is closing its border, it will only coast 1,200 euros for an adult. The children can ride for free," answered the short man cunningly.

Wait a minute ... Did I hear right? Are they making fun of us? Hello? We are refugees and not millionaires driving our Lamborghinis to Hungary! Who can offer 1,200 euros out of the cornfields?

"Twelve hundred what? No way! we are not paying such an amount, thank you," answered the man from our group.

"I know that the amount is large, but it will take more than two and a half hours driving to Budapest. Plus, you are safe in the taxis. The army and the police won't even notice you. From Budapest, you can take the train to Vienna directly, and then you can go to Germany, Denmark, or Sweden. Trust me, other smugglers will even ask for 2,000 euros for an adult and 800 euros for children," said the tall guy, trying to convince us.

They had a point. No one wanted to stay in Hungary. We just wanted to pass through. On the other hand, I don't think they were lying about the police forcing us to give our fingerprints. We'd experienced how they treated refugees. Still, 1,200 euros was an imaginary number to ask for.

"Don't agree, anyone," said Yazan in Arabic so the men wouldn't understand. "Show them that we don't care, and maybe they will lower the price."

We argued with the taxi drivers about the price until the short guy said, "OK, we can lower the price to 850 euros for an adult—no more and no less. We can lead you through a way where there is no police. We want to remind you that if you get caught, you will be forced to give your fingerprints and stay in Hungary, as the Dublin Regulation says. You don't want that to happen. Don't think of it as a ticket to Budapest only; it is a ticket to Germany, Sweden, or Norway!"

"What should we do?" I asked my brothers.

"Are you really asking?" said Amer. "All we have left is around 430 euros for the six of us. Definitely no!"

The group didn't take more than a minute to refuse the offer. The taxi drivers seemed upset that no one had agreed to get scammed.

"OK, you are free to do whatever you want, but we warned you. Good luck staying in Hungary!" growled the short guy before walking away with his friend. It is funny that people get upset when they couldn't scam us.

"The heck is wrong with these people?" said Sleman. "If I had 1,200 euros, I wouldn't have left Syria."

"Right? Now we need to continue walking before the soldiers come back," said Amer.

We continued shuffling behind Yazan and the other guys until there were no longer cornfields but jungle. Amer jogged to catch up with the guys, who were walking at a quick pace to make sure we were on the right track.

When he returned, he said, "I talked to one guy, and he told me that we are on the right track according to what his cousin explained to him. I don't know; I don't like it."

"Don't worry," said Mohamad. "We are walking in a big group."

"Walking in a big group can be a disadvantage," argued Haya. "We can easily get spotted and caught."

"Yeah, but at least gangsters won't attack us," added Othman.

"With a group or without, we have been walking for almost four hours, and we haven't arrived yet. Thank God it isn't raining," said Ghaithaa.

I was too busy trying to control the sounds of my stomach. I was hungry and had only a banana and a croissant.

"Look out!" I said quickly as I saw Yazan gesturing to us.

"Get down, everyone!" shouted Sleman.

We all got down immediately and didn't make a sound. Three army jeeps were driving fast from a distance. Seconds later, they were out of sight. We had no clue what was going on or where they were heading, but we were glad we weren't noticed. The sudden movement and the loud sound of the jeep engines woke Abdo and Linda up, and they started crying along with the other kids in the group.

"I am really afraid that the kids will expose us while we are hiding from the army," I said apprehensively. We were lucky this time, and I hoped we would get lucky next time as well, but we couldn't just rely on luck.

Everyone stood up again except for the old lady. She had damaged her legs and had a pulled muscle. Diyala helped her get up, and we were ready to follow the guys.

More and more trekking; it seemed endless. Our legs were rusty, and the heat wasn't going easy on us. It was time for a risky rest. We penetrated deeper into the forest and used the trees as a shelter from both the Hungarian army and the burning sun.

"Do we have any water left?" Othman asked.

"Half a bottle only," I replied.

"I have a small bottle, but I need to make milk for the toddlers," said Haya. "It is better if they drink their milk now while we are resting, and hopefully they can sleep after."

I shared the water with Othman and ate the croissant and banana I had left.

"Can you move now, Mother?" asked her son.

"My whole body is hurting, but I must move. May God give us the strength to continue," lamented the old lady while her son helped her get up.

"It will be better soon; just a little bit more," said her son with a warm tone.

Sadly, that fifteen minutes rest was nowhere near enough. However, resting wasn't the solution, so we had to keep going.

Half an hour later, we reached a narrow river, which we followed. The river was getting wider as we walked along with it. The guys stopped moving and were looking around for something.

"What is it?" asked Sleman after the families caught up with them.

"We have to cross this river," answered Yazan. "We are looking for a trunk or something that can be used as a bridge."

The river didn't seem deep, but it wasn't safe for the families to just cross it. After some searching, a badly shaped trunk was the best thing to be found. It was long enough to reach the other side of the river. Two guys crossed the river to help the families from the other side, while Yazan and the two other guys helped the families cross the river.

Women were the first to pass. While the first woman was on the trunk, the trunk started shaking; it was unsteady. The woman got nervous and stayed still until Othman and Amer held the trunk with their hands to keep it from moving.

Five women had already passed and the sixth was on the trunk when we heard a booming bark that scared her and made her fall into the river. We looked in the direction the sound had come from. It was the Hungarian army.

What the ...

"I said stop!" Another roar echoed in the forest. Birds fled their homes in fear.

"Run!" a guy shouted.

"Go go go!" Amer yelled as he gave me a push.

My heart started racing with my legs. I grasped Linda's stomach strongly, but she was way too shocked to cry.

Women were screaming in fear, and men were shouting instructions that no one followed. Screaming wasn't the only thing that was heard but barking as well. The army had dogs that chased us. Maybe this was how they found us in the first place.

Othman was in front of me; he had always been the fastest among us. Amer and Haya were running beside me, while Mohamad, who was holding Abdo, came last with Ghaithaa. It was a race with no finish line.

"Argh! Stop!"

A scream tore through me and had me looking behind. A soldier hit a man with a swagger stick on his leg and knocked him down. Then my eyes shifted to Ghaithaa, and I saw fear in her face. How did I forget? She has cynophobia—she is terrified of dogs.

Once a dog got near her, she immediately lost consciousness and hit the ground. Mohamad got down next to her. He kept the dog from biting her with one hand while covering Abdo with the other. Finally, the soldier held the dog, but he couldn't stop it from barking.

"Amer, Othman, stop! Mohamad!" Those were the words that escaped my mouth and made them realize we had to stop.

We got down on our knees in a sign of surrender. The soldiers knew that we had no intention of running and passed by us hunting those who hadn't surrendered yet. Within five minutes, the whole group was arrested—even the five women who had managed to cross the river. They wouldn't leave their families. But the two guys who crossed the river to help the women weren't among those caught. They seemed to have escaped.

Yazan, Sleman, Diyala, and everyone else were down on their knees. The soldiers stood next to us with their weapons behind them, talking over their handheld transceivers in Hungarian while looking and pointing at us. There were twelve soldiers in all.

I looked around at the group. The old lady hadn't run; she just stood still with her son. The woman who fell in the river was all wet and side-sitting; she was telling her husband that her ankle hurt. The man who was hit had some blood running from his nose, as the soldier had kept on hitting him in different parts until he totally surrendered. And of course, the kids were crying.

So this is how it feels to be illegal? I thought. *A couple of days ago, I had my rice and chicken plate, sat in front of the TV, and saw reported news about illegal migrants, only to change the channel to watch a movie. Now, at this very moment, I am one of them.*

10
A Hellish Ride
"My brother ... he is not breathing!"

With the permission of the soldier, we used some water from the group to wash Ghaithaa's face. She finally regained consciousness, but her face was pale and she had a headache.

"Are you OK, Ghaithaa? Did you hurt yourself?" Mohamad asked her anxiously.

She just gestured a yes.

I looked at the dogs. They were black and brown German shepherds with sharp ears moving around like satellites. I'd always adored dogs, but these were not cute. Not at all.

"Come on, get up!" a soldier ordered, gesturing with his hand.

We got up and waited for our next instruction.

"Move! Follow us!" ordered the soldier. He moved to the front of our group.

We followed his steps, with soldiers behind and beside us. We didn't go back from where we came; instead, we continued following the river. We walked until there was no more forest to find three army jeeps and a white and a blue police van with metal grates in the windows which two police officers were standing next to. Each was wearing a navy blue T-shirt, trousers with cuffs, a gun, and a handheld transceiver attached to a black belt.

We waited patiently for the soldiers to finish their discussion with the police officers.

"You, get in the van," said one soldier to the old lady.

"Can I go with her? I am her son."

"Yes, you get on too," said the soldier.

"But where are we going?" the son asked.

"Get in the van!" the soldier snapped.

"Yes, sir!" the son said, and he and his mother got into the van.

The guy who had been hit got in the van as well, along with his wife and child. The police officers had their last talk with the soldiers before getting in the van and driving away. Some other soldiers got in their jeeps and drove in the opposite direction. Four soldiers were left.

"Follow us!" a soldier called out.

Two soldiers walked in the front, and the other two were in the back, some distance away from the group.

"Man," Othman said. "Look at their weapons. Damn, I wish I could try them."

"You know that we are not playing Call of Duty, don't you?" I replied.

For some reason, Othman was excited to be arrested. He had a close look at the weapons he used to carry in video games.

"What will the soldiers do with us?" asked Sleman.

"I don't know. My first thought was that they were going to send us back to Serbia," Amer answered, "but it doesn't seem that they will."

"Maybe they will let us enter Hungary?" wondered Diyala.

"I hope not," said Yazan. "We will be forced to give our fingerprints. Didn't you hear what that taxi driver said? They are forcing people to give their fingerprints."

"Yes, he said Dublin law or something, but honestly, I didn't understand what he was talking about," Diyala admitted. "What is Dublin?"

"It is Dublin Regulation; an EU legislation that contains a list of criteria to determine which EU country is responsible for your asylum claim. The aim is to prevent people from seeking asylum in multiple EU countries. Often the first country where the asylum seeker arrives is responsible. Many countries don't want us, refugees, to enter them so that they aren't obligated to take us. This is why Hungary is sending people illegally back to Serbia. Compared to Germany or Sweden, Hungary is a poor country, and there are high levels of unemployment even among citizens."

"But we and everyone else got fingerprinted in Greece. Does that mean we don't have the right to seek asylum in other European countries?" I asked.

"It doesn't affect us," Mohamad answered. "The European countries close their eyes to it because Greece is almost every refugee's first destination, and it cannot accommodate everyone."

"But we didn't get fingerprinted in Croatia or Serbia, even though we entered both," Haya pointed out.

"Because they don't want us to seek asylum. In other words, we passed illegally with the government's permission," explained Amer.

"That is right. Guys, if we enter Hungary, whatever happens, don't agree to give your fingerprints. My friend who has been in Germany for a couple of months entered Hungary and was arrested, humiliated, and nearly beaten to death to give his fingerprints, but he refused," said Yazan. "After a week, they released him and set him free without him giving his fingerprints."

"Shh! No more talking!" snapped the soldier.

I had no idea about what was said. My excuse was that I was the youngest. I didn't have to know all of this. My brothers could take care of such matters. I didn't think it was that complicated, but the journey was getting harder day by day.

After one hour of walking along the razor fence under the heat of the sun, which the soldiers didn't mind, we reached a gate that many police officers were standing behind. The gate opened, and we were in Hungary. The soldiers had more talking to do with the police before they climbed into the jeep and drove off to chase fugitive refugees.

"We are moving," jeered a police officer.

We followed him and his comrade, not knowing what we would be forced to do but not expecting things to go well. We walked until reached a small village near Szeged. We were taken to a camp that was essentially a police station. It was similar to the police station in Greece where we stayed to apply for the white card, yet its square was more spacious.

The whole police station was surrounded by a high fence. We were let in the square of the police station, and the two officers that led us left without saying a word. Around twenty people were already in the square. They were probably a group that got caught.

"OK? What to do now?" asked Sleman.

"Look! It is the old lady's son. He arrived before us. We can ask him," I said.

"Excuse me, we are from the same group," Amer said to the son. "Did the police inform you what we should do here?"

"Oh, hi! No, the police didn't speak to us yet, but I asked a guy who was here before me, and he said that we will get fingerprinted. But I cannot find that guy now," the son answered.

"We might have to wait for hours," said Yazan. "I am going to see where we can get water."

"And I am going to find where the toilets are," I told my brother.

There weren't many police officers in the square, only three that were coming in and out of the police office.

I stopped one officer and asked, "Excuse me, where are the toilets?"

"There are no toilets," he said without looking at me and continued walking by.

I stood in my place wondering if I should ask another police officer who didn't look friendly. I decided that I could hold it for a little longer.

It was feeding time for Abdo and Linda. There was one issue: we had run out of powdered milk and water. There were no volunteers, and we couldn't go out of the police station. There was nothing we could do to stop their crying. They were hungry, and this is what toddlers do when they are hungry. With toddlers, the journey was a hundred times harder.

Yazan came back wearing a wide smile on his face.

"What?" we asked.

"First things first. A police officer is selling a single cigarette packet for twenty euros. Can you imagine! I am craving a cigarette, but it seems like I am going to quit smoking. Second things second: I think it is possible to get out of here."

"How?" we all yelled at the same time.

"Hush!" Yazan said. "Don't make a scene. I am not yet sure. But as you see, there are not many police officers, and the gate is left open with no guard. There are no guards outside the gate as well. Plus, the old lady's son said that he asked a guy and he cannot find him now. Don't you think that he just walked out of here?"

"Maybe we were told that we will be forced to give our fingerprints just so that people get afraid of Hungary and choose another path," I suggested. "Now that we have entered Hungary, why would they force us to give our fingerprints? They will just turn a blind eye to us, I think."

"Even if we get out," asked Diyala, "what are we going to do next? Where to go?"

"There is a small restaurant near the police station," Yazan told us. "We can ask the owner if there is any bus or train station that we can go to."

"So you are telling me that we are considering escaping again now?" Amer was hesitant.

"I mean, people have been here for hours without any interactions from the police," shrugged Yazan. "It is getting darker. This might be our only chance to get out of here."

"I am down for it," concurred Sleman. "But we cannot all get out together. We are nine. We need to go one by one."

"No," Amer protested. "If any one of my brothers gets caught, he will have to stay in Hungary, and we cannot just leave. We do it all together or we don't do it at all."

"OK, I will go first," said Yazan, volunteering to be the bait. "If you see me giving you a sign, follow me immediately. And remember, don't make a scene."

I was worried that the toddlers' crying would not allow us to sneak away, but other children were crying as well, which would cover us and might give us a chance. We watched Yazan walking in a roundabout way to the gate while keeping an eye on the police officers. He got out! We were shocked that he just walked out without anyone noticing.

We were already up and ready when he gestured to us. We started prowling slowly towards the gate and gradually increasing our speed. The seconds felt so heavy.

We did it! We were free, but there was no time for celebration. We had to keep moving until we were far enough from the police station. Yazan rushed to the restaurant to ask for directions.

"OK," he told us. "I asked the owner, and he said that there is a train station near here. There is a train to Vienna at 19:45. I checked the time on the wall clock, and it 19:20, so we better hurry."

"Amer, check if the owner sells milk," said Haya. "They have been crying for hours."

A minute later, Amer came out carrying two apples and a bottle of water. "He has no milk, only apples. We can mush the apples and feed them. Let's move now. We don't want to miss the train."

We had to move between buildings, watching out for the police. It was like playing hide-and-seek. An upgraded version where if we got caught, our lives would change forever. The train station wasn't too far, and we managed to reach it miraculously without being noticed.

"Oh my God! What is this?" fretted Diyala as she watched the long line of people standing outside of the train station.

"How long have they been here?" questioned Ghaithaa.

"I don't know," said Othman. "There must be a problem. Let's book our tickets first then ask. We got only fifteen minutes left."

"It will be hard to move around here," added Mohamad. "I will go with Amer to ask about the tickets. You stay here. Don't move; we cannot ring you."

It was impossible to buy tickets in fifteen minutes. Moving one step forwards alone could take fifteen minutes.

"Tickets? Do you need tickets?" a man with a broken accent asked me. I could tell by his uniform that he was a member of the train station staff.

"Yes! Yes, we do. Just a second," I told him. Then I shouted, "Amer, Mohamad, come back! This man is selling tickets."

They rushed back, and everybody bought tickets.

Are we going to fit? was the only question I needed an answer for. In my vision range, there were at least four hundred people. The train station was literally drowning in people. It felt so small and tight. Was it a spacious station to fit all these people? Or was it a small one? I had no idea. Heads were the only thing I saw.

Finally, people started moving. Seconds later, there was no longer something called a line. Everyone was scattered around the place trying to get onto the train.

"Move! Raise Abdo and Linda!" shouted Mohamad while covering Ghaithaa and moving forward.

I couldn't raise Linda on my shoulders, so I embraced her tightly and got pushed by the crowd from behind. Amer held Abdo, but I couldn't see them. It was so noisy and chaotic that I saw Sleman's lips moving but couldn't hear him, I could only follow his steps while being pushed in every direction. The screaming of Linda slapped me and awakened the beast inside of me. I always gave my place to others and waited in line; even if someone passed me without permission, I didn't mind. But this time was different. I had a crying 1-year-old holding her tiny fingers to her uncle's chest to get her out of this chaos.

I held her even tighter, bent my head down, moved with my shoulders, and kept battling until I reached the door. Othman, Amer, Haya, Diyala, and Yazan got to the train before I did. Sleman was standing at the door giving me his hand to grab. Other people were getting on the train through the windows.

"Where are Mohamad and Ghaithaa?" I slurred.

"They got in, but they had to move to the back," said Sleman.

We got shouted at and pushed to move to the back. We wanted to, but we couldn't. There was no space for an ant. The train was literally jammed. The guy next to me was stepping on my foot. The lady behind me was leaning on my back. I had to lean on Sleman's chest.

The train was delayed for about ten minutes until every person somehow got on it. The doors closed, and the train moved. I never thought I would be grateful for not having agoraphobia, the fear of crowds. Still, it was unbearable even for a social butterfly. I was crammed against the door with Sleman, with around twenty people between me and Amer.

I was worried about Linda. She wasn't the only one crying. Dozens of kids were howling in the narrow train, and all I could think about was *how did we end up here*. On land, I would give Linda to Haya or someone else, but on the train, it was impossible. She was my responsibility. Luckily, she was tired and hadn't slept in a long time, so getting her to sleep wasn't that hard.

How is it possible for this many people to be here? I wondered. *And how did the police let them and us go?*

I heard a conversation between two ladies.

"Thank God," said one. "After two whole days of waiting, the train is working again."

"Let's just pray it continues to Vienna," said the other. "I heard rumours that the Hungarian police stop the train to get people out of here and into camps. I have a bad feeling about this."

It was hard to convince myself in such a situation that we were lucky, but we were. People had waited for two days to get on the train, and we waited fifteen minutes. That also explained how so many people were at the train station. They had been gathering there for days. The conversation didn't just make me feel lucky but anxious too.

What if the police capture us? They, of course, do know about this train, but is there a chance that they will turn a blind eye to us? Or will they force us to stay in camps and give our fingerprints?

Negative thoughts kept fogging my brain. However, I wasn't able to move or think clearly. I had become a statue. An artist would be satisfied if I was his subject to be drawn.

"Mohi, try to turn around a bit," said Sleman.

He himself needed to change his pose, as I had been leaning on his stomach and chest for a good hour. I started turning around slowly, thinking I was bothering everyone around me. On the contrary, it gave them a chance to move their bodies as well.

The cracking sound of my bones was a disagreeable symphony of tiredness. Moving, the thing I wanted to do most, was nothing but pain. But my complaining time was over the second Linda woke up. She grabbed my shirt in a gesture that she needed to be carried properly. I lifted her up to my chest, and she started making noises. I hadn't appreciated those moments when she was asleep.

My legs felt like rocks. My paralyzed arms were holding an innocent crying toddler to my weak chest that was starved for air. My eyes saw nothing but curly thick black hair with dandruff and the dirty dark green shirt of the back of the guy standing in front of me. I examined every detail of him and discovered moles that not even his mother knew about.

Still, I couldn't adapt to the crying of Linda. I felt the real meaning of a headache. I was in a situation that I wouldn't wish on an enemy.

Suddenly but slowly, the train stopped.

"No!"

"What happened?!"

"Why did it stop?"

"It is over."

It was like being in the middle of a party where everyone nattered at each other, and I felt lost. The voices kept rising, and more participants joined the chatter until the train moved again. All of us let out a sigh after holding our breath, unleashing an increasing amount of carbon dioxide that was enough to make a hole in the ozone layer.

Our humble celebration didn't last long. The train slowed down again, and the black hair of the guy in front of me turned into red and blue. The doors opened, and people leaked out like water held behind a dam. I was pushed out and tumbled down to my covering Linda with my arms to not let her head hit the ground. I didn't wait for an apology; I just walked metres away from the train before I collapsed to swallow air.

Seven police cars besieged us in an arid field on a starless gloomy night. It was a maliciously played trick by both the police and the train company.

Despite knowing how abrasive the Hungarian police were, some people tried to run away. But they couldn't outrun the ruthless dogs. Others refused to leave the train but did by force.

"Where is Linda?" I heard Haya call out.

I gathered again with my brothers and listened to the police gibberish before four buses parked before us. According to the police logic, four buses could hold the same number of passengers as a stuffed train. We crammed with Yazan, Sleman, and Diyala on the same bus, like pickles in a jar. Two police cars drove along with the buses.

"Where are we going?" asked a man.

"I can't tell you," said the driver.

"Are you taking us to camps?"

"As I said before, I can't tell you."

Saturday/17-10-2015/04:23

"So?"

"Yeah, it seems like the bus is going to Croatia!" A guy on our bus used GPS to track our location.

Everyone was relieved after our nerves had burned with anxiety and fear. We were getting out of Hungary and not being sent to Hungarian camps, as I had assumed. The worst hadn't happened.

It was drizzling when we got off the bus. Both the sun and the moon were conquering the sky. Harsh cold wind slapped me in the face and chilled me to the bone after hours on a fixed-windows bus.

Abruptly, Mohamad hit the ground.

"Mohamad! Are you OK?!" Ghaithaa freaked out.

He was hardly heavily breathing. I looked around and saw a small tent with the Red Cross banner, and I ran there asking for help.

"My brother … he is not breathing!" I wheezed.

A volunteer ran back to Mohamad with me. He kneeled, checked Mohamad's pulse, and put his finger beneath Mohamad's nose.

"He is fine, but we will need to take him to a warmer place. Help me walk him to the tent."

I helped Mohamad walk while Ghaithaa followed me with the bags. Not everyone was allowed to accompany Mohamad.

"I suppose you are his wife," said the volunteer. "Does he have any health issues?"

"His health is fine, but he has breathing problems," answered Ghaithaa. "He used to work with a T-shirt heat-press machines for twelve hours a day and was constantly breathing hot air, and that affected his lungs."

"I see," said the volunteer. "Unfortunately, we don't have access to medicine here, but his condition is not dangerous. There is nothing to worry about. It probably happened because of the sudden change in the temperature from warm inside the bus to cold outside it."

"Do you have a bathroom?" I broke in.

The volunteer looked at me in confusion, but when he saw my *I can't hold it any longer* dance, he knew I wasn't fooling around.

After answering the call of nature, I went back to the tent to see Mohamad sitting in a wheelchair, wearing a heavy wool sweater and holding a cup of warm tea.

"The buses that are going to the camps are arriving soon," said another volunteer who had just walked into the tent. "People have to move now. I need some help arranging the lines."

"OK, I am coming," said the volunteer who had helped us. "Your brother should move now. I don't want him to wait longer here."

"Just give me a minute to look for my brothers outside," I said.

"They will follow you. Don't worry."

I pushed Mohamad in the wheelchair and followed the volunteer with Ghaithaa to the bus. The rain was getting heavier, and people were placing their stuff in the luggage and getting on the bus. I threw the bags in the luggage while Ghaithaa helped Mohamad to get on the bus. The driver started the engine, but I still couldn't find my brothers.

Before the bus moved, a police officer got on the bus to check that everyone was ready. I told her that I couldn't find my brothers, and we couldn't leave without them.

"Hurry and try to call them out," she said.

I got off the bus not knowing where to search. I had already searched all the places. I saw a line of people waiting for the buses, and I knew I would find them there—and I was right. They were standing in line with Yazan, Sleman, and Diyala when I shouted for them, but when I turned around, the bus had driven away.

I ran with my brothers waving for the bus but got stopped by a soldier.

"My sick brother and his wife are on that bus!" I fretted.

"The bus is already gone. You will have to wait for the next one." He pushed us back.

"Bu—"

"Stand at the beginning of the line so that you can take the next bus," said the soldier.

Not all the buses were going to the same destination. We might be sent to a different camp. Mohamad was barely able to move, and neither Mohamad's nor Ghaithaa's phones were working. We had a right to panic.

11
A Change in Plans
"You are my hero!"

We were sent to a military camp divided into two sections with a fence. Dozens of soldiers wearing camouflage uniforms, holding their assault rifles, were spread out at the entrance, near the tents, and all over the camp. Small and large dark-green tents were randomly attached to the ground, and because of the rain, everything was soaked. The ground was muddy, and the tents were engulfed with water that turned them into muddy swamps.

We searched every corner of the camp looking for Mohamad and Ghaithaa, but we had to surrender to the rain and find shelter first. Almost every tent we checked was full except for a small tent on a little high ground far away. We didn't waste any time occupying it.

"I am going to search for Mohamad and Ghaithaa," said Amer. "You stay here. Don't leave the tent, because other people will take it."

"The kids are freezing. Their clothes are wet," said Haya.

"Let's rub their bodies to warm them," said Diyala.

She and Haya rubbed Linda's face and hands. I rubbed Abdo's feet while holding him firmly in my lap and blowing out with my mouth to warm his tiny hands. Minutes later, Amer came back with a miracle.

"Oh, he found you!" Haya exclaimed.

He had found Mohamad and Ghaithaa. Mohamad couldn't walk steadily and had to lean on Amer. Othman and I put our jackets on the ground for Mohamad to lay on, and Amer covered him with his jacket as a blanket.

"What happened? How did you manage yourself with Mohamad and the bags?" Haya asked Ghaithaa worriedly.

"An Afghani family saw me struggling and offered to help me," Ghaithaa replied. "They carried the bags and helped Mohamad walk to a tent. I don't know what would have happened without their help." She added, "But Mohamad's temperature is high and he feels cold. His condition will only get worse if we stay here."

"Well, thank God there are good people on this journey and that we were sent to the same camp," commented Yazan.

"Mohi," Haya said, "let's go and ask some volunteers for clothes for the kids before they get sick."

The rain finally stopped when we got out of the tent, but the sky was still cloudy. I carried the toddlers and looked for a volunteer. We met a lady volunteer from the UNHCR.

"Excuse me," Haya said, stopping the lady. "Are there any clothes for the toddlers? All their clothes are wet."

"I think we have some left. Please follow me."

We followed her to a UNHCR tent, where Abdo and Linda got dry clothes. The clothes were worn out and much bigger than their size, but sufficient to serve the purpose. The volunteer also filled the bottles with milk after washing them. Getting dry clothes and milk bottles filled was all that Haya had wished for. Her eyes were sparkling. Her soul was happy.

On our way back, I heard my name being called.

"Look, it is Mohi!" It was Laith and his family. "What are you doing here?"

"Laith! Glad to see you again!" I said. "We have just arrived."

"Did you find a place to stay in?" Laith asked.

"Yes, come with me," I told him.

I showed him the way to our tent and introduced him to Yazan, Sleman and Diyala. Laith explained that it wasn't so crowded when they applied for the white card in Greece, and they were able to take the ferry to Athens in the afternoon. They were one step ahead of us, but they had spent two days in the forest trying to enter Hungary. When they couldn't, they came to Croatia.

"I am going to die if I don't eat right now," said Othman. "I am famished!"

He wasn't the only one starving. My stomach was growling. We hadn't had lunch for two days. The women stayed in the tent with Mohamad and the kids, while the rest got out to get food. There was a long line that ended at a UNHCR tent.

"Thank you," said Amer after getting a small rounded orange can and two slices of brown toasted bread. "Can I also take for my wife? She stayed at the tent."

"Um … OK." The volunteer wasn't sure.

"If you want, I can bring her here," said Amer.

"No need for that. I believe you. It's just that there isn't enough food, and you know, some lie about getting food for others. But here. These are for your wife."

"I understand; it happens. Thanks!"

We plodded back to the tent through the muddy ground to find that the women had used some plastic bags as a carpet to sit on.

"What is this?" asked Sarah, examining the orange can.

"It seems like … maybe it is a fish paste?" faltered Laith. "But how do we eat it?"

"The bread is crispy, so just dip it and eat," said Yazan.

Ghaithaa tried to feed Mohamad, but he wasn't feeling good and refused to eat anything. A can of fish paste wasn't enough to fill the void in my stomach, but it was definitely better than nothing.

"I am going to ask about when and how will we be moving," said Laith.

Yazan and Amer followed him and came back with bad news. They'd heard rumours that Hungary and Germany had closed their borders. We might have to stay in Croatia for a couple of days until there was a solution.

Othman asked to use Laith's phone to call Ezz; as his phone needed to be charged, and see if he heard something about the rumours. He found out that Ezz had just arrived in Austria and hadn't heard about Germany closing its borders. Hungary, on the other hand, wasn't allowing people in in the first place.

I got tired of waiting for updates. I walked out of the tent and looked for a volunteer to ask. I saw a volunteer wearing the blue UNHCR uniform and a paper with her name on it: Ivona. She had pale skin, captivating green eyes, and black hair in a ponytail. She was scurrying from place to place. I hesitated to ask her, but I needed to know.

"Excuse me," I said, stopping her. "Can I ask you something?"

"Yeah, sure!" she replied.

"I heard that Hungary and Germany have closed their borders. Is that true?"

"Actually, I am investigating this," she told me. "I heard about Hungary closing its borders, but I am not sure of Germany. I'll inform you as soon as I get new updates. Where are you staying?"

"In that tent over there," I said, pointing at our tent.

"OK, got you. What about you? How are you feeling? Are you alone or with your family?" she asked in a friendly tone as she put her hand on my shoulder and tilted her face.

"I am fine, thank you! I am with my brothers and their wives. We have two toddlers who are feeling cold. The weather is so harsh."

"OK, don't worry. I'll take care of them. I'll see what I can do for them."

People started gathering around us, and I didn't want to get her into trouble for answering my unending questions. "Anyway, thank you," I said.

"OK. I will come to you later." She understood my intention and nodded.

I didn't expect her to interact with me in such a way, especially since she seemed busy. I went back to the tent and waited nervously for the smallest piece of news. *If the rumours are true, how many days are we going to wait in Croatia? Could it be weeks? Will we be forced to stay in Croatia? Ugh, isn't there rest in this journey?*

Ivona's voice disrupted my anxiety. "Hello! Good, I could find you. Can I come in?"

"Yes, of course," I said.

She came in and kneeled. "Well, Hungary did close its borders," she confirmed, "but the borders of Germany are still open. Now there is a new plan being studied: you will go to Austria through Slovenia instead of Hungary. In my opinion, this is good news. The Hungarian police are not so friendly, and we've heard many stories of people who got beaten by them. On the bright side, you will be among the first to go through Slovenia, which means camps and clothes are prepared for you."

"I guess it is better this way," I said. "Thanks for telling us."

"Can I ask why the camp is divided with a fence?" said Sleman. "I see people on the other side too."

She explained, "When the buses arrive, people on the other side of the fence will move out, while people on this side will move to the other side of the fence. It is for organizing the numbers that are leaving." She added, "By the way, Mohi told me there are toddlers here. How are they?"

She asked some questions about their health and played with them a bit. Before leaving, she asked if we needed anything. Amer asked if she could get him a better pair of shoes, as his were ripped, causing water to get into them.

"I'll try to get you a better pair of shoes, but please don't tell anyone," she said. "We have a limited amount of clothes, and the priority is for those who are in need."

She came back ten minutes later hiding the pair of shoes under her jacket. Then she left again to take care of other people. Having someone this nice was all we needed after everything we had been through. Our hearts were shattered into pieces from seeking a moment of peace and not finding any.

The ground was still wet in our hellish tent, but it didn't matter because I was wet as well. I lay on the plastic bags and took a nap.

"Mohi, wake up, we are moving to the other side." Ghaithaa nudged me.

"Wh … What … other side?"

I heard Ivona's voice. "I will talk with the soldiers to open the gate for you, but as I said, you need to move quietly. If people see that the gate is open, a big crisis is going to happen, and the soldiers will have to act."

"Ivona will take us to the other side," Ghaithaa explained. "We need to follow her. Now get up."

We waited for a signal from Ivona. Once she reached the gate, she waved at us to start moving. We prowled separately, pretending to look for a place to stay, and the dark was our ally. I doubted that some people saw us, but it was over. We got in, and the gate closed after us.

"We cannot thank you enough," said Sarah.

"There is no need to thank me. I couldn't let the kids stay in the cold for another day. Hopefully, three or four buses will come tomorrow to drive people to Slovenia, so whenever they arrive, you need to leave everything and catch a bus. Hopefully, you will be able to leave for Slovenia tomorrow."

The other side had two large military tents with lightweight camp beds.

"Haya, Ghaithaa, and Diyala, bring the toddlers and follow me, please," said Ivona.

She led them to a container room that had an electric heater, beds, and blankets. She led them to heaven.

There wasn't much lightning in the camp, and the sky was covered in black clouds. We entered a tent with Yazan and Sleman, while Laith's family was taken to the second tent. Only two beds near each other were empty, with one blanket to use. Mohamad lay on a bed, and we covered him with the blanket and put our bags on the other bed. Amer, Yazan, and Sleman arranged plastic bags on the ground to sleep on, using their jackets as blankets. I threw my body on the other bed and buried myself in the bags before sleep pooled on my eyelids.

Othman wasn't feeling sleepy. Instead, he went to the container room where Haya and Ghaithaa stayed to drink water. Abdo was being naughty, and when he saw his uncle, he waved his hands in the air to get carried. Othman sat with Abdo on a little rock near our beds and mumbled some songs. While he was singing, Ivona was passing by and heard him, so she sat next to them and sang along while playing with Abdo.

"I know it is a harsh journey, not only for the toddlers but also the women and men, but it is going to be OK," said Ivona.

"I believe in that," said Othman. "Thank you for your kindness."

When the night became colder, Othman returned Abdo to his mother and lay down beside Amer.

Sunday/18-10-2015/08:11

I woke up to the whistling of the biting wind that blew underneath the bed to reach my inner bones. I woke up every five minutes to hug the bags and cram my body against the bed to warm it. This was the chilliest night so far. I pushed the bags away coming out of my grave and sat for a moment holding my head to prevent my throbbing brain from escaping—to feel the tension of a good headache. Mohamad was still sleeping, but none of the other guys was inside the tent.

I put on my stinky shoes, zipped my jacket, and walked outside. Everything was foggy. People looked like shadows. I took a deep breath, and my lungs screamed in pain. The air was bitterly cold and made my whole body shiver.

"Did you eat yet?" Amer walked over to me.

"No, I just woke up."

"Hurry to that tent over there. There aren't many people waiting in line."

He was right. If I went now, I might not have to wait for hours.

The water in the mud was frozen. The sound of breaking ice was heard clearly as I walked. Besides the tent where the UNHCR was giving food, there was another tent where people could get clothes. I got the same can with the fish paste and a slice of brown toasted bread.

"Sorry, my brother is sick and can't come here," I said. "Can I get some food for him?"

They were kind and gave me the same for Mohamad. I hurried back to the tent, but Mohamad wasn't there.

"Where is your brother?" I asked Othman.

"He woke up feeling better and went to search for a better pair of shoes than his," said Othman.

"OK. Did you eat?"

"No, I don't feel like eating. I got this beanie for you."

I put the beanie in my bag. I sat on the bed, opened the can, and dipped a crumb of the toast in the paste. But before I could put it in my mouth, Yazan stormed the tent.

"The buses are here. Come quickly!"

"Go find Mohamad and bring him with you!" shouted Othman. He took all the bags with him.

I jumped out of bed and ran to the clothes tent to see Mohamad standing in a line.

"Mohamad! Come! The buses arrived!" I hollered.

I drew the attention of a hundred persons. It was like I threw a grenade and scattered the crowd. I ran with Mohamad in a race with people, but before I had reached my brothers, soldiers formed a barrier of troops, blocking us from getting through.

"My brothers are there! Please let us through!"

I took a push as an answer.

"Can you please let these two through? Their family is here." It was Ivona. She saved us once again.

"Thank you!" I said.

"Hurry and stand in line with your brothers," she replied.

Yazan, Sleman, and Diyala succeeded in making it through with the rest. However, Laith's family wasn't around. As Ivona mentioned, there weren't enough buses for everyone, and the soldiers had to control the crowd to prevent chaos.

"Excuse me, we are going to Slovenia, right?" Othman asked a volunteer.

"There are only four buses at the moment. You will either go directly to Slovenia or the train station and take the train to Slovenia afterwards."

"No! Not the train. The toddlers can't take it anymore!" moaned Haya.

Before we got on the bus, Ivona came to wish us safe travel. I wanted to thank her. I knew words weren't enough, but they were all I had.

"I can't thank you enough, Ivona. You are my hero!"

"No, you are the hero. I am not. It is your life, your story, and you are your own hero." She held my hands firmly and smiled at me.

We got on the bus and waved goodbye to Ivona, a rare heart that cannot be forgotten.

12
A Shame
"You have a problem?"

An overloaded SWAT officer wearing all black and holding an automatic rifle as if he was about to go to a world war got on the bus and didn't leave the driver's side. Needless to say, Othman swooned with delight examining his uniform.

I couldn't let go of our fear of the train. I didn't want to experience that ordeal again. I just wanted an obvious answer to end my suffering.

"Are we going to the train station or Slovenia?" I asked the SWAT officer.

"I have no information. Please go back to your seat," he replied bluntly.

I didn't expect to get a lollipop from him. I just wanted a hint.

"This is it. We are going to the train station," sighed Yazan after we saw the train station.

Another train. I wasn't sure if I ever wanted to disappear from life so much.

"Wait, the bus isn't slowing down …" Ghaithaa said.

I kept biting my nails until we were far enough from the train station. We just passed by it. The bus didn't stop. We were as happy as clams at high tide, yet the struggle of the bus was still present. The windows were shut, and the air was running out. I explained to the officer that my brother was sick. He opened a window for five minutes to ventilate the bus before shutting it again.

Three hours later, we reached the Croatian–Slovenian border and were told that we were going to change buses.

"Mohamad?" I asked. "Are you OK?" He was inhaling heavily from his mouth. He leaned against the bus and fell down to his knees. By good luck, a police officer rushed to help. He made Mohamad sit forward to help him breathe properly and instructed him to calm down and inhale and exhale slowly. We stayed by Mohamad's side until the officer assured us that he was OK.

Meanwhile, the police had finished inspecting people's bags, and it was our turn. I emptied my cross-body bag on a white piece of fabric for inspection, and when the officer had done his work, we were ready to head to the bus. Ghaithaa informed the driver of Mohamad's condition and asked him not to turn on the heat, and we finally met a driver who actually listened to us.

We drove all the way to Dobova city in Slovenia. I was lucky to sit by the window this time instead of Othman to witness the charming view. The water drops on the window couldn't dim the vibrant red adobe roofs of the ancient buildings and the grey brick stone street surrounded by hundreds of trees that were fighting for the survival of their yellowish leaves.

We stopped at a police station. A UNHCR volunteer helped the police officers organize the crowd. When he passed by us, Ghaithaa told him that Mohamad couldn't stand for a long time because he was sick.

"Both of you can come with me. You don't have to wait," said the volunteer.

Before getting in, people were given blue wristbands. As explained, those who had blue wristbands were the ones who would take the bus to Austria the following day.

Next to the police station was a big building and a spacious garage.

"We will open the door of this building. Women and children will go in, while men can stay in the garage," said a guy over a loudspeaker.

"Haya, here, charge my phone," said Amer. "I am sure there are outlets in there."

"Charge mine, too," said Othman.

Haya, Ghaithaa, and Diyala followed the volunteer to the building with the other women and children. Inside the building, it was like a basketball stadium, with a high ceiling and camp beds and covers.

"Can I get some help bringing some beds out, please?" the volunteer asked us.

Othman, Yazan, and four other guys helped to bring ten camp beds but didn't bring blankets, as there were only a few. The beds were put next to each other so that more people could sleep, although many would have to sleep on the ground.

I had to use the bathroom and found a blue plastic toilet booth in the corner of the garage. For the first time of the history of this journey, it was clean—in other words, not used yet. I told my brothers to use it before it got dirty.

Two UNHCR volunteers moved around and gave each one of us a can of fish paste and a slice of toast. When night fell, the rain stopped. Gradually it became quieter. The building door opened slightly, and I heard a woman calling me while half of her body was behind the door.

"Hey, young boy, come here," she gestured.

"Yes?" I asked.

"Don't look in; women took off their hijabs. You know what, it is freezing out there, and we have heating inside. So here, take these blankets for you." She handed me some blankets.

"No, it is OK. Cover the kids instead. Don't worry about us."

"No, you take them. The kids are warm. Take these and come back to get more," she insisted.

Before sleeping, we had a late-night talk about the war and what happened to the Syrian people. We even questioned the existence of humankind. Mohamad wasn't sleeping but lying on a bed. He seemed to be better but not fully recovered.

"Sleman, you are the only one who didn't share his story," said Othman. "Why did you decide to come to Europe?"

"I need to go to the bathroom," he said. "I'll tell you later."

Amer gave Othman a nod to stop talking.

"What? Did I upset him?" Othman asked.

"He doesn't like to talk about it," whispered Amer. "His wife was exposed to verbal abuse and sexual harassment from the military, and he was threatened with death for hitting a soldier. When he comes back, change the subject."

Sleman came back feeling embarrassed, but Yazan saved him with his humour.

"You know what?" Yazan said. "I started to like this fish paste. It is better than my mother's cooking."

After we finished eating, we lay on the bare ground, and every two persons covered themselves with a blanket. Some didn't cover themselves, including Amer and Yazan.

Monday/19-10-2015/07:56

We got up early. A backache was the only thing I felt, but I was more than happy to lift my back off the ground. I asked one of the volunteers who roamed around about going to Austria, and he told me that buses were coming in the afternoon to drive us there. Haya, Ghaithaa, and Diyala came out of the building with Abdo and Linda to get some fresh air.

Later on, more than five buses arrived at the police station. With the help of volunteers, the police organized the crowd and let them on one by one after giving each a yellow paper wristband.

"Isn't that Sarah waving at us?" asked Ghaithaa.

"Yes, it is her!" said Diyala.

They got their wristbands and scurried to us.

"Where were you, man? We were worried about you!" said Amer after shaking hands with Laith.

"Ugh, don't ask. We were thrown on the train."

"I hope it wasn't that bad," said Haya.

"Not that bad?" Sarah retorted. "We stood for hours in the train with no space to sit. We couldn't move our toes. The woman who was stacked next to me lost consciousness. I don't know what happened to her, but paramedics rushed to help her and many others, and there was that guy who …"

I walked away slowly to avoid unneeded trauma.

"People who got here yesterday, who have blue wristbands, please follow me," said a volunteer hours later. "And for those who have yellow wristbands, buses will come to pick you up tonight or tomorrow."

"Wait, can we come with you?" Laith asked Amer. "We don't want to spend the whole day here."

"I am not sure. Let me talk to the volunteer."

We stood outside the police station waiting for the buses. They hadn't arrived yet, but both the garage and the building were overcrowded, so they wanted to vacate the place. When the volunteer asked to see our wristbands, he saw that Laith and his family had yellow ones.

"We have blue wristbands. This family has yellow wristbands, but they can they come with us?" asked Amer. "We have been together all the time but got separated in Croatia."

"They can get on the same bus if there are empty seats on the bus; otherwise, they will have to wait," replied the volunteer.

Four buses arrived minutes later. Everyone who had a blue wristbands got on the buses, and luckily, there were empty seats for Laith's family.

At sunset, the bus stopped at a huge single-storey building surrounded by soldiers wearing brown and green camouflage uniforms. We were confused. We had been told that we were going to Austria, but it didn't seem that we had left Slovenia. I went with Mohamad, who was feeling refreshed, to ask the soldiers for an explanation.

"You are still in Slovenia," said the soldier.

"When are we going to Austria?" Mohamad asked.

"No idea."

We were led by soldiers to the building. It wasn't only huge from the outside but the inside as well. It had plenty of tables attached to benches. It was a military dining hall. The other part of the building was for sleep. A line for food was formed before we realized, but we decided to reserve a place for sleep first.

All the beds were military bunk beds, and we arranged six beds close to each other. Amer, Laith, and the women weren't feeling hungry, so I went with the rest to get some food.

They were serving pasta with creamy mushroom sauce. It was hot and smelled delicious, especially after having nothing but a can of fish paste.

Finally, cooked food! There were no empty places to sit, so we took our plates to the sleeping hall. Within seconds, I was licking the plate.

"*Assalamu alaikum.*" A man approached us with his wife and two young boys. "Can we sleep in these empty beds here?"

"Yeah, sure," said Sleman.

After a while, we heard a distracting loud noise echoing in the hall. It was three guys dragging three bunk beds towards us.

"Hi! Can we put these beds next to you?" they asked. "We are Syrians."

"Yeah, it is fine," answered Laith.

One of the guys whistled and yelled for his friends. A group of six guys grabbed beds in the hall and put them next to ours. The beds were stacked and left our beds with no way out. There wasn't enough space to get in or out of the bed but to climb.

"Hey, excuse me, brothers, what are you doing?" Laith interrupted them.

"What do you mean, what are we doing? We are arranging the beds to sleep. You have a problem?" said a guy as he put his hands on his waist.

"Of course I have a problem. At first, you were only three, and now you are nine. Do you expect us to jump over each other to get out of our beds?"

"Well, we are not moving from here, whether you like it or not," sassed another guy.

"Don't make up problems. Just take the beds and find somewhere else," said Mohamad.

"You shut up. I am not talking to you." A guy pushed Mohamad.

"Try to lay your finger on him again and see what will happen." Amer jumped in front of the guy.

Yazan, Sleman, and the Syrian family that had joined us stood their ground too. We had a staring contest for a good minute before they decided to retreat.

"And we were happy to find Syrian families. I swear that animals are a thousand times better than you," a guy spat. "If we were in Syria, I would have stomped you under my foot."

"Too bad to see you forced to be civilized," Othman fired back at him.

What a shame. Fighting instead of being united. This shouldn't happen.

The hall was quiet again after the show. I lay down to sleep in the bottom bunk while Othman lay down in the top bunk. I tossed and turned for an hour in bed but couldn't close my eyes. My stomach was hurting, and I felt nauseous.

"Mohi, are you OK?" Haya noticed that there was something wrong.

"I don't know. I feel like I am going to throw up." I put my hand on my throat.

"Is it because of the pasta? Go ask some volunteer if they have medicine."

"I don't know. I'll check."

I am not a food expert, but I could tell that the pasta was swimming in oil before it was served. So much oil was used for cooking. It was shining. I went to the food hall and explained how I felt to a volunteer.

"Unfortunately, we don't have medicine here. But we have pills to lower the body temperature. It might help you feel better."

Please, not pills. Pills were my biggest enemy. I didn't know how to swallow those little devils; they gave me hard times. I wanted to ask if they had syrup instead, but it didn't feel right. He gave me two pills and a cup of water. I didn't want him to see me struggling with the pills, so I sat outside the building.

OK. It is simple. Just put it in your mouth, push it back with your tongue, and swallow it. You can do this.

I took a sip after a sip of water, but the pill was still in my mouth refusing to leave it.

OK whatever. I shrugged before I took the last sip and chewed the pill. I felt instant regret. It was so bitter that I bleached out. My whole body shivered. *Why am I like this?*

I had been planning to take the other pill, but no, that wasn't going to happen. The pill made me feel worse. I stayed near a trash can preparing to vomit, but I couldn't. It was cold outside, and I couldn't fight the weather.

I went back to bed. Lying down didn't help, so I sat on the bed for hours before I eventually fell asleep sitting.

Tuesday/20-10-2015/07:04

Buses were waiting outside the building. Because there were so many people, we were told that some would have to wait until noon. We woke up early and were able to get on the buses in the morning. The guys we'd argued with the day before weren't around. Probably they couldn't catch the morning buses.

The bus dropped us off at a shelter only a few kilometres away. We booked two tables, and I went with Othman to ask a UNHCR volunteer what was our next step.

"You are going to Austria," he answered.

Around 08:30, a police officer said over a loudspeaker that we were moving in two groups. The first group was for the families and would leave at 09:00, while the second group was for the guys and would leave at 13:00.

"Othman, Mohi, and Yazan, stick to us in the family group," said Laith.

People started gathering next to the exit to leave with the first group. When it was time for the first group, the exit opened, and people charged towards the door—guys before families. The first group was supposed to be for the families, but explaining that to the scrambling crowd wasn't a solution. Amer held Linda on his shoulders, and Othman carried Abdo in his head, while I held Haya's hand and fought our way out.

When the police saw the chaos, they immediately closed the exit.

"Othman, Mohi, Ghaithaa. Is everyone out?" Mohamad looked around.

"Yes. They all made it," answered Sleman.

A police car was waiting for us outside the shelter. A police officer told us to follow the car as she led us slowly. We were around a hundred people walking behind the police car.

Subsequently, we reached a small town named Gornja Radgona, and we were so eye-catching. It was raining lightly, and the group was wearing plastic raincoats in blue, green, and yellow. The villagers couldn't ignore the colourful folks that were moving. Some were secretly taking photos. It was a free fashion show.

We continued walking until we reached a bridge on the river Mura connecting the Slovenian town of Gornja Radgona with Bad Radkersburg in Austria and stood in a line that ended in a military tent.

"You are from Syria, right?" a soldier wearing a brownish-green uniform with the Austrian flag and an olive beret asked us in Arabic.

On our way with the group to the Australian border

"Yes, we are from Syria. Are you Austrian?" replied Amer.

"I am originally from Egypt, but I came to Austria when I was a little kid."

"It is our pleasure to meet you," said Amer.

"My pleasure. I am really sorry about what is happening to you and your country."

"Uh … What can we say … Anyway, what are we going to do here?" Amer asked.

"You will wait in the tent until the buses arrive to drive you to a camp," the man said. "That is all I know."

There wasn't one big tent; instead, there were several small tents that were connected with one another. It was warmer inside the tents, but the ground was all muddy. Soldiers were pouring us hot tea to keep us warm. They had no idea when the buses were coming, so they told us to rest a little. While drinking the tea, I saw a bus coming from afar.

"Hey, there is a bus coming," whispered Diyala in a low voice. "Let's move and be the first to get on it. We don't want to be in the back of the line again."

Quietly, we carried our bags and walked outside the tent to greet the bus. Three buses came to drive us to the next camp, and for the first time, we were the first to get on a bus and sat in the back seats. Compared to the other buses that we took, this bus was a paradise. It was warm inside, and the seats were comfortable and roomy. I sat next to Othman, and before the wheels on the bus even began to spin, he fell asleep.

"I wish I had your brother's superpower; to sleep anywhere, anytime." I told Mohamad, who sat behind me with Ghaithaa.

After the change from cold rainy weather to a warm and quiet place, my body muscles relaxed, and within minutes, I fell asleep. My wish may have come true.

"Mohi! Mohi! Look through the window!" Mohamad nudged me.

I opened my eyes slightly, and my vision was still not clear. The bus was in a tunnel, and I could only see the light at the end of it. When the bus left the tunnel, my jaw dropped to the floor. Amazon-green meadows stretched to the left and right of the long highway. Clouds were underneath us. Red barns with brown and white and black cows decorated the endless green hills, and faraway white mountain peaks jutted into the sky.

"I swear, for a moment, I thought I was dead and in heaven!" I answered with my mouth open.

"How I wish I was a cow living here!" jested Laith.

"That's it. I am staying in Austria," said Yazan.

It was one of the most beautiful views my soul had ever witnessed. It was just like the cartoon shows that I used to watch as a child.

The road seemed endless, and Linda was being grumpy. She was bored from being on the bus for so long, so I carried her and tried to brighten her mood a little.

Three hours later, the bus stopped at a giant one-storey building in a mountainous area. We all got off the buses. There were Syrians, Afghanis, and Iraqis. We walked to the building, but the main door was closed. There was a little bell that we rang, and a volunteer from the UNHCR responded, opened the door, and said, "Hello! Please come in!"

When we first got into the building, we saw many volunteers from the UNHCR and the Red Cross preparing food on tables in a long wide corridor.

At the end of the corridor, there was a huge, spacious hall with plenty of navy-blue inflatable air mattresses with built-in pillows. There were some people already in the hall, but it was so big that it looked empty, and our voices echoed. We moved some mattresses for us, Yazan, Sleman, Diyala, and Laith's family.

"Oh God ... it is so comfy!" I howled as the mattress absorbed my body.

We were so glad that we didn't have to sleep on the ground or on two-centimetre-thick mattresses. Laith's boys, Adam and Yosef, started running around and playing in the hall while Abdo and Linda burst out in laughter trying to catch them crawling.

"Look! What are these people carrying?" Sarah was concerned.

We saw people carrying towels and small plastic bags. Laith went to investigate and minutes later came back with a towel and a plastic bag that contained a little plastic

Linda and Abdo playing on the mattresses

shampoo bag, a toothbrush, and a mini toothpaste.

"Hurry and get these. It is not yet crowded!" he said.

"Finally, some hygiene products," said Yazan.

Laith stayed with the kids and the bags, and the rest of us went to get what he got. I then started looking around for a toilet. There was a small staircase in the back of the building. I went down it and walked a little to find three green plastic toilet booths next to each other. They weren't so clean but not so dirty either.

In front of them was a small individual room with no door. I checked it and found it had one shower and three sinks. The room was empty; there was only an Iraqi guy who was taking a shower. I thought it would be my best chance to wash my hair right away. I rushed back and took the towel and the shampoo.

"What are you doing?" Othman asked me.

"There is a room with sinks. I want to wash my hair. Come, people haven't found out about it yet," I answered.

He followed me with Mohamad, but when we got there, there was only one sink available. Toothbrushes and shaving blades were all over the place.

"Should we go back?" I hesitated.

"Nah. I haven't smelled shampoo in decades. You are not in a five-star hotel. Plus, you should come here an hour later and see what this place will look like." Mohamad convinced me.

We decided to use the same sink and lined up behind each other. I only had a little bag of shampoo, and I wanted to make the best out of it. I took off my shirt because I didn't want it to get wet. I put the towel around my shoulders and soaked my hair with warm water. It had been over a month since I last got a haircut, and my hair was long enough to donate it.

I tried giving my hair a massage but ended up scrubbing the hell out of it. It was greasy and clumpy and sticking together. I then used half of the shampoo bag and scrubbed it again, but it didn't seem to make a big difference. I used the rest of the shampoo and scrubbed my hair again. I probably needed at least two more shampoo bags, but I was happy to finally wash my hair after so long. I rubbed my hair with the towel vigorously to dry it before putting on my shirt. I got out of the room, and people were already waiting impatiently to wash their hair.

"I'll go back to the hall. It is cold out here," I told Mohamad who was waiting his turn after Othman.

I hurried back to the hall while rubbing my head with the towel.

"Oh man, I feel so fresh!" I said.

"How is the place?" Amer asked.

"If you want to wash your hair, you have to go there immediately. Five minutes later, the place will be chaos."

"No thanks. Being bald has advantages, boy," he bragged as he rubbed his bald head proudly.

"Easy for you. What should I say?" said Haya, laughing.

One thing I know for sure is that women's hair requires much more shampoo than men's.

After a while, Othman came back, and Mohamad followed after. We all were together except for Yazan, who then came holding two toast slices, a single-serving packet of jam, a single-serving packet of butter, and warm lentil soup in a plastic cup.

"They are serving food. Go get some!"

We got in the food line one after another and ate together.

"You know what? We have made our decision. We are going to stay in Austria," said Sleman unexpectedly while we were eating.

"For real? Weren't you planning to apply for asylum in Germany?" asked Mohamad.

"That is right. Everyone I met advised me to go to Germany, but I really like Austria," conceded Sleman.

"There are beautiful views and cows in Germany as well," joked Laith.

"No, I am not staying because of that," giggled Sleman. "My aunt has lived here for fifteen years, and also my wife has relatives here who can help us in this new country."

"So we are going to say goodbye soon, aren't we?" I sighed.

"I am not going to say goodbye, Mohi. I am going to say thank you," said Sleman softly. "Thanks to all of you for coming into my life. I have only known you for five days, but I got to know you for a lifetime."

"In all honesty, we have never met people as friendly and trustworthy," added Diyala.

"Ugh, Diyala, I am going to miss you so much. We have become a … family," said Haya.

"Come on, you guys! It is not like we won't be able to see each other anymore. Sleman and Diyala, you are both welcome to visit us in Sweden whenever you wish," said Amer to break the wall of sadness.

"You have a home in Germany as well," Sarah added. "I wish you the best in all that you do."

After eating and washing my hair, and with the air mattresses, there was nothing to do but to lay down and take a sweet nap. I curled up on the mattress and let myself drown in it under the short blanket that reached but my ankles. It was annoyingly cosy at first, and I kept switching sides before I got used to it. Compared to the harsh pavement and muddy ground, though, the mattress was with no doubts a five-star service.

Finally, a moment of peace and relief, I whispered to the world before my eyes shut for a desired break.

13
A Walk Through the Night
"They died."

At sunset, I woke up coughing. I tried to close my eyes again, but I couldn't sleep. My body had gotten used to sleeping for short periods only, even if it wasn't enough.

"Othman? Are you awake?" I asked after seeing him moving.

"No," he mumbled.

"Let's ask the volunteers about when we are leaving."

"Why would you ask them? Let them take their time. This place is a palace."

"The bus window is more comfortable for you. Get up," I ordered.

He had to surrender and get up at the end to free himself from my nagging. The rest were still asleep, but I could tell that they wouldn't hold up sleeping much longer. Some people in the hall were awake, but the hall was surprisingly calm.

We approached to two volunteers from the Red Cross who were drinking warm tea and having a conversation together and asked them about our departure time.

"You will probably leave tomorrow morning, but we are not certain if you will go to a second camp or directly to Germany," one of them answered.

I got worried about being sent to another camp. Getting to Germany was one huge step. Still, deep down, I felt kind of glad to sleep on those mattresses for another day.

There wasn't much to do, especially when the rest were asleep, so we decided to take a walk outside the building. The coughing came back again. I assumed that it wasn't a big deal, and I just happened to cough. I kept convincing myself that I didn't have a cold, but sickness doesn't go away by pretending to be fine.

Of course, when we are finally at a comfortable place, it is time for a cold.

Before we got out, Othman poured tea for both of us. I zipped up my jacket and put on my beanie that Othman got me in Croatia. I had learned my lesson. We walked out the door to find a guy about Othman's age standing out holding a cup of tea. I had glanced at him while walking in the hall after washing my hair but we hadn't talked to each other. He was one of the first arrivals to the building.

"Hi," I greeted him and shook his hand. "Mohi."

Othman introduced himself as well.

"Hi, I'm Hasan," he replied. "Nice to meet you."

"It is freezing out here, right?" I said. What else to talk about but the weather?

"That is right. Do you want to walk around a bit? Moving will warm us up," he suggested.

"Yeah, why not?" said Othman before we traipsed through the cold night.

"So, Hasan, did you come here with your family or alone?" I asked.

"Not really." He smiled before answering.

"That means your parents are still in Syria?" guessed Othman.

"Yeah, you can say that. I lived in Aleppo with my parents. I was an only child. Our neighbourhood wasn't safe; in fact, it was raided multiple times. Each time, the army would arrest some men for unknown reasons. My father was once arrested, but thank God, he got out alive after two months. I was 16 and couldn't take responsibility for my mother alone."

He continued, "Most of our neighbours fled their homes and migrated to Turkey, as it was the nearest safe country. My father didn't. He had a soap factory, and he refused to move to another country and lose his business. Anyway, one day my father came back home and told us that we were moving to Libya. Of course, I wanted to get out of Aleppo at the earliest opportunity, but when it was inevitable, I was in shock and fear. By the way, are you OK with getting away from the building? I mean, if you want, we can go back," Hasan asked.

"Don't worry. Go ahead—continue," said Othman. I agreed.

"OK. My father changed his mind three months before I turned 18, the age for military service, you know. He was afraid that I would get killed or kill someone. He started making phone calls to a Libyan friend of his, and they planned to start a local joint project. However, my father had unfinished business regarding his factory in Aleppo, and he needed some time. He decided to send me to Libya before him and my mother. His friend promised to take good care of me until my father followed me to Libya. I did as my father planned and travelled to Libya."

We stopped at a red traffic light to let a car coming from afar pass. We weren't in a hurry, after all.

"They died," Hasan said. His voice became shaky, and he sniffled.

Oh my goodness. I stopped myself from gasping and coughing and tried to console him.

"I am so sorry to hear that. May God have mercy on him." I tried to look him in the eye, but he was looking straight at the ground.

"How I wish I was with them when the bomb dropped on the house," Hasan said. The pressure of his tears was higher than his dam of pride, and he let his salty tears break through.

"I don't know what to say, man," Othman said before realising that the best thing to do was not to talk to Hasan.

We continued walking in silence through the black night, headed nowhere. It was cold, and I hated it—yet the cold was our only company. It forced our brains to think of something else besides sorrow and forced our bodies to shiver. We walked alongside Hasan. We were beside him physically but miles apart emotionally.

The moonlight was hiding behind a blanket of dove-grey clouds and couldn't wash away the amber light from the soaring street lamps highlighting the three of us as foreigners in a foreign street we never thought we would meet at.

"One of our neighbours called me and told me what happened one week after I travelled to Libya," Hasan finally said, breaking the silence and rescuing me from choosing the appropriate words to say in such a situation but failing.

He continued, "When I first knew that my father and mother died under the rubble of our house, I lost my mind. I'd never experienced grief this bad before. I was at the home of my father's friend. I went crazy; I screamed and shouted. I smashed the door of the apartment, jumped down the stairs, and ran like a maniac in the streets. My father's friend followed me with his wife to calm me down, but I started cursing them. In the end, he caught me, hugged me close to his chest, and restrained me in the middle of the crowd.

"When we got home," he added, "I told him that I wanted to go back to Syria, but he refused and hid my passport. I flew into a fit of rage over him controlling my life, but he did it for my own sake. What would I do in Syria? Even if I travelled back to Syria and wasn't dragged into the military right away, I had no one left. None of my relatives were in Aleppo. Some had fled and others died."

When we reached a rotary, we changed our direction and headed back towards the building. I wished we had done that earlier, but I couldn't interrupt a guy who had lost his parents for a silly cold of mine. I knew that I had caught a cold already.

"I ended up working in his supermarket," Hasan went on. "He was a kind man who took care of his friend's son, but everything has an end. The situation in Libya got worse day by day, and he had to shut down his supermarket after an economic crisis. I had to find a new job and a place to stay. I got a job in a fast-food truck during the daytime and slept in the truck at night. I saved up some money, you know, to start a new future.

"After I had been saving up for five months, an armed gang showed up at night and tried to coerce me into giving them all I had. When I refused, they attacked me, stole my money and my phone, and destroyed the fast-food truck that I worked in. I went back to zero again." His tone of voice wasn't sad anymore; instead, it sounded heated.

"Damn, could it be worse? What did you do next?" Othman said in excitement. It was interesting to hear the story knowing that Hasan made it out alive.

"The gang threatened to hurt and kill me if they saw me again. I thought of going back to my father's friend, but I would have been a burden. I made some online friends, and one of them lived around a city called Sabratha in western Libya. I went to an internet cafe and explained everything to him. Even though we had never met, he cared a lot for me and offered me a place to stay until I found a new job, Mohi, are you sick?" he asked as I coughed for the tenth time.

"No, I am fine. There is just something in my throat. Don't worry." I pretended to be OK. We were on our way back anyway, and I wanted to see how his story would end.

"OK. Where were we? Right, so I moved to my friend's apartment, and he helped me to get a job in a small restaurant. The salary was so low, but the good thing about my job was that I didn't have to pay for my food. I worked there for one year. I went through a rough time and encountered countless atrocious racial attitudes. The idea of committing suicide didn't leave my brain. I thought and made scenarios of how people would react and who would care.

"One night, I was walking near the coast of the city looking at the sea, and I got the idea of fleeing to Europe instead of giving my life up. If died, at least I would die trying. I searched for smugglers. I had many questions, but when I asked for the cost, which was 700 dollars, I changed my mind. After one year of work, I could only save around 450 dollars.

"Day by day, the idea of fleeing to Europe grew bigger, and I became more determined. When I finally could save 700 dollars after working extra shifts, I called the smuggler, and he told me that the cost had increased to 1,000 dollars. I was desperate; so lost. I hated everything and everyone. I just wanted to die. By the time I saved 1,000 dollars, the cost would have increased again.

"I had to speak to someone. I had no one but my friend. I met him I talked about everything. I cried, I sobbed, I cursed. I did everything I could think of. I lost every hope in this world."

He was indignant, and his tone of rage got sharper. "Thank God I got to know that friend. He decided to lend me as much money as he could offer, and in turn, I kept searching for other smugglers, hoping they had cheaper prices. Some asked for 1,300 dollars and others for even more. I finally found a smuggler who asked for 1,000 dollars and told my friend. Fortunately, he could secure the missing 300 dollars."

Our walk was coming to an end, as we were slowly approaching the building and could see it from afar. "Two days after, I found myself loaded onto a decrepit old fishing trawler with a sea of crowd, surrounded by the great Mediterranean Sea. The smuggler promised that it was going to be a safe and easy voyage. Of course, I didn't trust his words, but I never thought it would be as bad. More than two hundred people in an ancient rusty fishing trawler; I bet it was taken out of a museum. We balked at getting on it, but the smugglers, afraid that someone would tell on them, drew their guns and aimed them at us to force us to take the boat with nothing but life jackets. Fifty people were a lot to be on in it, and we were way more than that, including elderly people, pregnant women, and children. We had to leave our bags and stuff on the coast before getting on the boat. Guess how many days we stayed in it," Hasan questioned us.

"How many days? I thought hours! Two days?" Othman guessed.

"Nine," Hasan replied with a smile.

"Nine days? Are you kidding?" I was perplexed.

"I swear, nine days and nights in the middle of the sea. No food and no water. Not even a toilet. Some guys could sneak in some canned food and water bottles to the boat. We lived on a crack of bread and a sip of water a day, but everything was consumed by the sixth day. All I can remember after that was hanging my head out of the boat and throwing up. My body temperature fell. I was dehydrated, and I still have haemorrhoids. I was a lifeless dead body. I wished that I had committed suicide; it would have been easier. But that was not in my destiny after all."

We slowed down as we reached the building and stood under the door's rain cover.

"Anyway," Hasan concluded, "an Italian coastguard vessel came to the rescue. It was a moment full of hope, but I didn't have tears to cry. Everyone loves to have a safe decent life. I am a human after all." He smiled.

"Indeed," Othman concurred.

"And here I am now, in Austria, with the both of you. Life is crazy isn't it?" he chuckled.

"One day you are at your warm home, surrounded by your family, the other day everything is gone," I said while I blowing in my hands to warm them up. "Hasan, I know that the previous years have been the worst, but you are almost there. To be honest, I can't imagine how I would do if I was in your shoes, but you did it, and you survived." I tried to cheer him up. I knew that words could make a difference and have an impact on our souls, but in his situation, I doubted it. But they were all I had to offer.

"Thanks a lot, Mohi and Othman. This is the first time I have talked about my story to anyone. It is like I threw away a heavy burden from my heart. It made me feel lighter. Thank you!" he said and gave us both hugs.

"You are welcome, man," said Othman. "Now listen: get a warm cup of tea and go to sleep. Try not to think about the past, OK? We will see you tomorrow."

Amer, Mohamad, and the rest were awake, sitting on the mattresses, getting Abdo and Linda to sleep.

"Where have you been?!" Amer said sharply.

"Relax. We were just walking around outside with a guy we met." Othman acted cold.

"You walked with a stranger in a country you don't know at night? For real?" Amer asked with a raised eyebrow. "At least tell us before you do so. We tried to call you, but you left your phone here."

"OK, sorry," Othman apologized after realizing that Amer had prepared a long speech.

I pursed my lips together, and a cough helped me prevent my laugh from spreading. The contradiction between Amer's irritating behaviour and the way Othman is unbothered has always been obvious. Amer wasn't satisfied, but he decided for the first time to not make a big deal.

"Mohi, did you catch a cold?" Haya seemed worried.

"I don't know, maybe," I murmured.

"And you were walking in the rain?" She frowned at me.

Here is Amer's feminine version, I thought.

"Did you ask the volunteers for medicine?" asked Haya.

"No," I answered. "But I still have a pill from the previous camp to lower the body temperature. I need to go to the toilet first."

I pretended to go to the bathroom, but I planned to throw the pill in the trash. I would never make the same mistake again and chew a pill, ever. I got back and found out that she had a cup of warm tea for me. She ordered me to dry my hair and get under a blanket.

Haya was taking care of me, and I appreciated it, but it made my heart break. My mother was the first person I thought of. No one could ever replace her.

Be grateful, I whispered to myself. *At least your mother is alive and didn't die under the rubble, and you can call her anytime you want.*

I looked around as I sipped the warm tea and saw my brothers busy with nothing but spreading the blankets. Yes, I was in a horrible situation, but I should not let it bring out the worst of me. Hasan had no one to trust or rely on, while I was rebuked for not saying I was going for a walk. I should be thankful for having a cold, not haemorrhoids.

A volunteer walked in and asked if it was OK to turn off the lights, and she did so after people told her to. The hall became dimly lit in an instant, with a faded light coming from the back door of the building. Gradually, the place became more peaceful. The cold had me exhausted, and its only benefit was to get me to sleep within seconds.

14
The Bridge of Despair
"The. Boy. Is. Bleeding!"

Wednesday/21-10-2015/07:34

We were waiting for the police to lead us to the train station at the main entrance after a perfect and comfortable night's sleep. Earlier, the volunteers had informed us that we would take the train. Everyone was worried, but the volunteers promised us that it was not like in Hungary.

"Here it comes," said Yazan, pointing at the police car we were waiting for.

"Good luck, guys!" said Sleman. "God knows how close to my heart you have become."

"Our journey won't be the same without you, Sleman! Take good care of yourself and your wife," said Amer.

"We are waiting for your visit. Take care!" Diyala said, shedding a tear.

Sleman and Diyala stayed outside waving to us until they faded into the distance. People who were willing to seek asylum in Austria stayed inside the building, to be moved to a migration centre where they could get fingerprinted.

In the early morning, I spoke with Hasan. He wanted to continue to Germany, but his health was terrible, and he couldn't sleep at night. He had been told to see a doctor for a check-up for his health, so he would be staying in Austria for some time. We had an early goodbye.

I hope he finds peace for the rest of his life, I thought as we left him.

The police car took the same road we had walked with Hasan the night before. It didn't look as dreary and dismal in the morning as it had in the night. The calm, clear sky was serene, with light fluffy clouds floating freely along with the birds. We passed the traffic light, and no one died. Unlike the driver the night before who'd had a long day at work and passed us in a hurry to get to his bed, today's driver seemed to be on a vacation, sharing his good-mood music list with us.

Thick trunks in soft yellowish-green dresses turned the gloomy lifeless street into an avenue, and a small coffee shop welcomed its daily customers for a hot cup of coffee, announcing the beginning of a new day. High buildings in the distance let their windows reflect the bright blue colour of the sky. All had been hidden in the darkness of night—an agreement between day and night to turn a blind eye to the stories that were told in the rain.

I was about to believe we weren't walking on the same street we had walked the night before. The freezing weather was the only similarity. *How come some days are dark, bitter, and spitting rain, and others are calm, lively, and elated?*

Before oppressing the darkness and accusing the day and the night of participating in some kind of conspiracy, I saw that the trees, the coffee shop, and the buildings were still in their places. It was the heart that decided to go blind to noticing the beauty around it. It was the drained heart that strayed from the right road.

The volunteers weren't lying. A silvery and shiny red train was waiting for us. Unlike the Hungarian nightmare, this train was empty and spacious. The aisle was wide, and the distance between the blue comfortable seats with armrests on both sides was enough to spread the legs in ease.

"Ugh, finally, one country left," said Laith as he leaned back in his seat and stretched his body.

"Not for us," said Mohamad. "We have two more countries: Germany and Denmark."

"Why don't you stay in Germany?" asked Yazan curiously. "I mean, Sweden is a good country for refugees, but Germany is good as well."

"You are right," agreed Mohamad. "But we have already decided to go to Sweden. We compared both countries, and we think Sweden is better for us."

"Amer, what are you doing?" I asked. He seemed busy with his phone and was not paying attention to the conversation.

"I am checking the direction of the train using GPS, making sure it is going to Germany," he said with his eyes on the phone.

Abdo and Linda started to get noisy. They were bored with sitting.

"Here, give me Abdo," Ghaithaa told Haya.

She and Othman sat on empty seats on both sides of the aisle, holding the toddlers near the window as they entertained them with the moving trees and flying clouds. After one hour of seeing nothing but spacious fields and rolling hills, Abdo surrendered to sleep in Ghaithaa's lap, seconds before Linda fell asleep in Othman's. Amer and Haya were the happiest parents on earth at that moment—a moment of peace and relaxation and, hopefully, half an hour of sleep before the toddlers' battery were charged up again.

I sat far from the others to avoid infecting them with my cold. I sank into the seat, covering myself with my multiple-use leather jacket. One hour later, my sleep was distracted by an unpleasant fishy smell. I opened my eyes to see two guys eating tuna. I covered my mouth and nose with my hand while coughing. The smell of the oil alone made me uncomfortable, and I knew I had to get away from the smell before I threw up.

I headed to the toilet at the end of the passenger car and tried to open the little window in it after I washed my face. It was stuck, but I managed to open it slightly. That pasta dish I'd had in Slovenia was still haunting me. I thought that I was OK after that night, but it seemed like I couldn't tolerate the smell of cooking oil. It was associated subconsciously with a feeling of queasiness.

"Mohi?" Mohamad knocked on the toilet door. "What is the matter?"

"Did the guys finish eating tuna?" I asked from behind the door.

"Is that why?" He sounded sarcastic. "Yes, they did. You are safe now."

"Says the person who can't breathe," I sneered. "Anyway, how much time left until we reach Germany?"

"Amer checked, and there are still three hours left," answered Mohamad as we walked back to our seats.

The hours passed quickly in comfort, and then it was time to disembark. The doors of the passenger cars closed behind us, and the train accelerated until it faded away, leaving us with two police cars that we were told to follow. Walking didn't bother us anymore; we had become used to walking miles and miles. Everyone was getting thinner on this journey—or ready for the Olympics, one could say. We swam and walked for countless hours.

We arrived at Salzburg, a city on the Austrian-German border. At some point, it felt like we had reached the centre of the city—a city that felt so warm despite the blowing cold wind that was desperate to reach our bones but getting blocked by the brownish-yellow and grizzled-grey old yet solid buildings that were terraced with red bricks.

Countless grey cobblestones mirroring the grey clouds fit together like an oversized jigsaw puzzle. The scent of freshly grounded black magic beans travelled from the many cafes to meet the aroma of baked white magic in the crisp air.

Buildings weren't the only thing in that city. Staring eyes were present too. Although they weren't hard to notice, it seemed like I got used to being stared at. I felt like a celebrity surrounded by a hundred bodyguards and police officers—an unwelcome celebrity. People weren't scrambling or shouting my name, but I was thankful they didn't throw eggs at me.

We passed through the city. The strong smell of magic weakened slowly, and the watching eyes rolled down on the photos taken of us. We reached a three-storey old building where the Red Cross staff was waiting for us.

"Hello and welcome!" waved an old man from the Red Cross staff.

"Hi! Is there a toilet?" I asked impatiently.

"Yes. It is at the end of the first floor."

I found myself in the toilet before I could thank him. I think he understood. He must have been in the same situation before.

"We are waiting for instructions, so you will have to wait here for a while before going to the German border. Hopefully you will be able to enter Germany today," I heard the old man saying as I returned from the toilet. Then he headed back to his colleagues.

"So? We will wait?" I said.

"Yes, and we are not sure for how long, so let's find a place to rest," said Amer.

We walked up the stairs to the first floor. The corridor wasn't roomy and led to three rooms with no doors. Each room had two beds, a sink, and an undressed large window that faced another building. We waited in the room near the stairs for a sign to go. Laith's family waited in the room next to ours while Yazan stayed downstairs with many others.

"Guys, come on, we're moving!" Yazan called out to us after two long hours. "We will follow that one Red Cross staff member. He is leading the way," added Yazan as we walked out of the building.

As the group walked on the smooth grey stones between the colourful buildings, the music of our feet on the streets played a chaotic rhythm.

We turned the corner to see a vertical brownish old concrete building with a tall black steeple that ended with a tiny bell and a weather vane detecting the direction of the wind. A big golden-blue clock at the top of the building pointing to 13:25. Eight parallel windows decorated the building, ending with an arch connecting the streets.

The building was easily sticking out among the rest. I was too busy trying to even the weight of Abdo with the bags on my back to ask what the building was, but I could tell it was a church.

"This is the border bridge between Austria and Germany," said the Red Cross staff after we passed the arch. "The German police are at the end of it. Form a line on the side of the bridge, and they will let you pass. I can't accompany you. Good luck!"

The line reached half the bridge, and we were in the back of the line with Yazan and Laith's family. The side of the bridge was separated from the two-way road by a low fence. It was above the wide Salzach River.

No buildings were around us to protect us from the wind that we had to face for half an hour without taking a step forward.

"What are they saying?" Yazan asked a man in front of us in the line.

"They are not letting people in."

"What? Why?" asked Yazan, hoping for a reasonable answer.

"I don't know. The guys say they closed the borders and are demanding that we go back to Austria." The man sounded desperate.

"This can't be true! That man from the Red Cross told us that there was a group of people who were before us, and they entered Germany. I don't believe that they decided to close the borders just now," protested Sarah to Laith, as if he was responsible for what was happening.

"You are right. There must be something wrong. Let us wait and see," replied Laith.

We waited for a whole hour until it started drizzling. People who were first in line started passing by us.

"Where are you guys going?" Mohamad asked one of the guys.

"We are going back to talk to the Red Cross staff. They won't seem to let us in," the guy answered.

"Should we also follow them back?" I asked.

"Yes. They are not letting us in, and it has started raining. The kids will get sick," said Laith as he held the hands of Adam and Yosef.

We strode back to the Red Cross staff, and they were shocked.

"The border police said that they closed the borders, and no one will enter Germany," one guy explained to the old staff member we first met.

"This is strange!" the staff member said. "We didn't get such news. The borders should still be open."

"That was what we were told," the guy informed him.

"OK, you can wait here for a bit until we investigate the situation," said the Red Cross man. He picked up his phone to make some calls.

"What if it is true? What if the borders are actually closed?" worried Ghaithaa.

"We heard the rumour when we were in Croatia, but Ivona said it wasn't true," I said, trying to reassure myself and the rest. "Let's just wait for what the Red Cross will say."

I sat down on the stairs with Abdo sleeping in my lap, waiting for the old man's response. Linda was awake with her mother.

The old man showed up after half an hour. "Sorry I am late," he said. "The borders are still open, and there is nothing official about it being closed. It is probably something the border police made up. Go back there and don't leave until they let you in."

"What if they refuse to let us go through again?" one guy asked.

"They might try, but you will get in for sure. Trust me," said the old man.

We went out of the building and headed to the bridge for another attempt. The music of our feet became familiar. I hated it. It was like a song killed by being played on repeat so many times that the brain couldn't stand it anymore.

I looked up at the big golden-blue clock to see that it was almost 15:00. I realized how much darker the clouds in the sky had become. I also noticed the nonstop spinning of the weathervane. We stood in a line on the bridge again. This time, we were in the middle of the line.

"They are saying the same thing. They won't let us get through," said Yazan after what he heard from the people in front of us.

"Hey! Everybody!" a man shouted. "Don't move an inch from here. We will stay here until they let us in!"

"Yeah, we are not leaving!" shouted another guy.

Like everyone else, we decided to wait. There was no way back and no solution but to wait. Cars were moving slowly on the bridge. Each car was stopped and searched, most likely for people illegally crossing the border into the country.

After half an hour of waiting, I felt a raindrop hit my neck. What were we missing, standing on the bridge with a beautiful view? Rain, of course! I held

Abdo between my stomach and knee, pulled out my beanie from the pocket of my jacket, and put it firmly on my head.

Abdo started to make noises, as he was uncomfortable. I made sure to swaddle his body with a light blanket and cover his face slightly, but he kept trying to break free. I moved around a little while patting his back gently, but to no avail. During the journey, I had become a little expert on how to deal with a crying baby, but this time Abdo wouldn't calm down.

"Here, give him to me," said Haya.

We waited for over an hour, and the line didn't move at all. We were all wet, and sitting on the pavement of the bridge was no longer something to worry about. The rain got heavier, the wind got rougher, and the river was flowing strong. Since we had left the building for the second time, the sky had been getting darker, and the weather kept getting worse. The police officers were watching us from under a rain shelter tent and drinking warm tea.

"Dad, I feel cold." Adam grabbed Laith's hand.

"Here, let me wrap the jacket around you and Yosef," said Laith as he took off his jacket.

"Abdo won't stop crying. I don't know what to do anymore," whimpered Haya in a shaky voice. She was about break down.

"Give him to me," said Amer. He tried to calm the boy down, but Abdo's crying only got louder.

"Let me carry him. Let me try," said Sarah.

Another child's crying beat Abdo's. He seemed to be yelling in pain. The child had somehow fallen and hit his head on the fence of the road, and he started bleeding immediately. His parents freaked out and rushed to the police. Their expressions and the repeated "please" were obvious signs that the police had no hearts.

"Goddammit," mumbled Othman on his way to the police.

"Where are you going?" Amer's question was ignored.

"Excuse me," said Othman in a loud voice. "The boy is bleeding. Can you let the family in?"

"No one is allowed to enter," answered the police officer with a cold look on his face.

"*The. Boy. Is. Bleeding!* Don't you see the blood covering all his face! I see a Red Cross tent only ten metres from here. Just let them in. He is a child!" shouted Othman as if he was the police officer. The parents waited desperately for the approval.

"There is Red Cross in Austria as well. Go back there!" sassed the officer as he exchanged looks of anger with Othman.

Another police officer joined the argument. He had a short conversation with his comrade in German and said, "OK, get in!"

Without hesitation, the father carried his bleeding child and rushed in, but the mother was stopped.

"Only one of the parents goes in. You stay here." The officer blocked the mother from going with her child.

"Come on! I am not staying here for one more second!" a man snapped. His wife tried to calm him down, but he wasn't listening to her.

"God damn them," he continued yelling as he walked back towards us. "They are treating us like animals. They are scum. What was I thinking of coming all the way here? How I wish I had died in my land before being treated like a dog by some low-lifes ..." He kept raging and cursing until his voice faded away.

We were upset and at a loss, not knowing whether to go back to the Red Cross building again or do what the old Red Cross staff member told us. When you are cold, wet, hungry, exhausted, and have crying babies, giving up is the easier option.

"I can't," Haya cried out of both emotional and physical exhaustion. "I can't take it anymore. Abdo won't stop crying. He has been crying for half an hour non-stop. I am afraid his belly button is going to explode. I have no idea what to do …" Her throat felt swollen, and she stuttered as she tried to speak.

"No, he is fine. He is just cold and having colic," said Ghaithaa, hugging Haya to try to calm her down a bit. Instead, Haya burst into tears.

I didn't think it was colic and wind. Abdo had been crying and sobbing for so long he had run out of tears. His crying made us and nearly everyone in the line nervous.

"Should we go back?" Amer asked, hoping someone would change his mind.

"Let's wait just a little more," said Laith.

I crossed my arms, leaned on the fence, and stared at the raging river. A while later, the sound of the water hitting the rocks became clearer and woke me up from my unpleasing meditating. Abdo had stopped crying, yet his deep shuddering sobs went on and on. I wasn't sure if he had fallen asleep, but he was finally calm.

"Look! It seems like they are letting people in!" Yazan bubbled.

People were indeed passing the border slowly. We were elated, after we had lost our hope and questioned the decision of this journey. We were no longer feeling cold. The excitement melted the cold away.

We stood up, picked up our bags that were lying on the wet ground, and came closer and closer to the police. Then we heard people warning that the police were forcing them to give their fingerprints. Whoever passed the border would have to stay in Germany. That meant we wouldn't be able to continue to our final destination, Sweden.

"What is that now?" sighed Mohamad.

Many people planned to seek asylum in Germany anyway, including Laith's family and Yazan, but not everyone. Some people chose to retreat and stay in Austria, and others were hesitant, just like us.

"What should we do?" Amer vacillated.

"I don't care anymore," said Haya wearily. Her face looked pale as a ghost's. "I just need all of this to be over. I was crazy enough to put my kids in a rubber boat. They are tired and sick. If they force us to give our fingerprints in Germany, we will give them whatever they want."

No one argued back. The idea of having to cross to more countries was painful. A part of me still wanted to be in Sweden, but I was so dead tired that I buried Sweden under my million thoughts.

When there was only Yazan and a guy ahead of us, Yazan turned around and said, "Unaccompanied minors are being taken to a camp for minors. Be careful, Mohi. If they ask you about your age, say that you are 18, OK?" Yazan warned me before the police officer asked to see his passport.

He asked for the passport! I had a panic attack. *The officer will know that I am under 18. What should I do? What should I say?*

The option of staying in Austria was no longer available. Yazan, Ghaithaa, and Mohamad had passed, and I was standing in front of the officer praying he wouldn't notice me.

"Your pass," the officer extended his hand.

"Here." I gave it to him.

"So, how old are you?" It was the question I never wanted to be asked.

"I am almost 18," I said hoping that I wouldn't be considered a minor.

He read through it and looked me in the eye. "Yeah, you seem so, you are alone?"

"No, I came with my brothers."

"You are fine as long as you are with your brothers. Here." He gave me my passport back and asked for Othman's.

I had a mini heart attack. I didn't know that having a guardian was enough to let me through.

A group of minors was being taken care of by a police officer and Red Cross staff in an opposite tent, and people who had their passports checked were sent to a bus waiting outside the rain shelter tent. I stood next to Mohamad and Ghaithaa waiting for the rest, but Mohamad told me to go before them.

I got on the bus but was stopped by the driver. "Are you here alone?" He looked suspicious.

"No, I came with my brothers. They are right there, but I feel so cold, I can't stay out longer."

"OK," said the driver.

The bus wasn't full, and the seats in the back were empty. I reserved them for the rest of my family. Minutes later, everyone got on the bus, and we all sat in the back seats. The police officers seemed to have lied about forcing people to get fingerprinted.

I noticed that Yazan wasn't on the bus. "Where is Yazan?" I asked.

"He was taken with a group of guys to another bus. I have no idea why," answered Amer.

"Call him then."

"I can't. My phone's battery is dead."

"I think we will meet him in the next camp we are going to," said Othman.

I looked around, and it was easy to notice that only families were on this bus. Since Yazan was taken with other guys to a different bus, I had a feeling that we wouldn't be going to the same destination, but I chose to stick with

Othman's optimistic thought. We waited some time for the bus to get full before it drove away.

It was dark when we arrived at our destination, another one-storey spacious building filled with wooden tables and chairs. Police officers standing at the entrance of the building welcomed us with cold faces. We watched many people getting out of the building and getting on buses that drove them into the night. We had no clue what was going on.

The building was nearly empty, with only us and the other people we were with on the bus, so finding an empty place to sit wasn't a drag. We sat on a table next to an outlet so Amer and Othman could charge their phones.

"Did you see Yazan between the crowds that got out of the building? He is nowhere to be found," asked Laith while scanning the building curiously.

"No, I didn't. My phone is working now. I'll call him," said Amer. "Hello, Yazan! How are you? Where are you? We couldn't find you," said Amer with the speaker on.

"Hi, Amer! I tried to call you, but it seemed like your phone battery was dead. Anyway, I was sent with other guys to a stadium, and now they are making us clean it," giggled Yazan.

"For real?" asked Amer.

"Yeah. What should I say?" said Yazan. He sounded both happy to have finally made it to Germany, where he'd planned to go, and upset at being treated badly. "But you knew that I would seek asylum in Germany. I have some friends here who can help me with work and such stuff. I just want to say thank you to each one of you. We created a unique bond and went on a journey that we will tell our children about."

"Well, we have children, and they were on the same journey we were on, so speak for yourself!" Laith cracked a joke as usual.

"You had to do it didn't you?" laughed Yazan. "I'll see you later. We might be neighbours. Amer, Mohamad, Othman, Mohi, and my sisters, I wish you a safe journey. Remember that you have a friend and a brother in Germany. Now, if you excuse me, a police officer has been scowling at me for too long now. I have to go back to cleaning. Stay safe!"

I couldn't imagine that this was how we were going to say goodbye to Yazan, the first person we met on this journey. He was a single guy who could have easily left us, joined another group of guys, and moved smoothly, not having to worry about a crying child or a tired woman. Still, he decided to stick with us, and he hadn't hesitated to offer his help.

I wanted to say goodbye, shake his hand, give him a hug maybe. But deep down I was happy. Saying goodbye over the phone was much easier, with less sadness to consume. Still, we were about to say goodbye to not one person but a family.

"So, here we are. Our journey is almost finished," sighed Laith.

"Your last stop," said Amer.

"Yes. We can't even think to continue further," Laith said.

"Do you remember the first day on the Turkish island when you decided to go back?" I asked, reminding him of the first time we saw each other. "You didn't just come back, you drove the boat and made it to Germany. Can you believe it?"

"It is all written in our fates. I tried to change fate, but I couldn't." He looked at me and smiled.

Laith wasn't a random person we met on the journey. He was the person who drove our rubber boat. Our lives were in his hands. He remained calm and made wise decisions in the most stressful situation one can encounter. If it wasn't for him, our journey could have ended differently.

"Come on, stay in Germany. We can be neighbours. How awesome is that?" Laith made another try at convincing us.

"What do you think?" Amer asked us.

"Germany is good, but you know that we decided to go to Sweden," answered Mohamad.

"I know, but it is easier to find jobs in Germany."

"Amer, we talked about this before," Mohamad interrupted.

"OK then," said Laith. "I should start asking what to do now and where to go. You were the best thing to happen in this journey and my life. I am so glad I got to meet every one of you."

The same fate that gathered us forced us to say goodbye—a forced goodbye, the very kind I hate. I stood on my toes to hug Laith, kneeled to hug Adam and Yosef, and waved goodbye to Sarah, who did the same after crying a river with Haya and Ghaithaa. We watched them talking to a police officer before they faded away, waving warm goodbyes from afar.

"Let's ask when the buses will arrive to pick us up," said Othman. He went with Amer to find out.

Ghaithaa wasn't OK, and I wasn't surprised. After waiting for hours on the bridge in the non-stop rain and howling wind, sickness was to be expected. She'd had an upset stomach since we arrived at the building. Mohamad went to ask a police officer if there was medicine or anything that could help.

"I asked a police officer," said Amer. "She said that the buses will arrive in twenty minutes."

Seconds later, Mohamad came back telling Ghaithaa to go with him; there were Red Cross volunteers that could help.

"No, wait, the buses are coming soon," said Amer. "We have to be here when they arrive."

"I am fine. It is not serious," said Ghaithaa to Mohamad, who gave up on convincing her to go to the volunteers.

We sat on the table not talking to each other. Othman and Amer were charging their phones. Haya and I were putting Abdo and Linda to sleep. It took us but two minutes, they were so tired. Ghaithaa was leaning her head against Mohamad's shoulder while putting her crossed arms around her belly. We waited for half an hour. The buses should have arrived, but they had not shown up.

"This is it. Come on. Let's go to the volunteers to see what your problem is," Mohamad told Ghaithaa.

"Can't she endure the pain a little longer?" Amer insisted. "We don't want the buses to come when you are not around, or we will be separated."

"She waited for half an hour in pain," replied Mohamad.

"Mohamad, listen to me and wait. We will take her to the volunteers the very first moment we arrive at the next camp."

"That could be five hours!" exclaimed Mohamad.

They kept on arguing. Amer had a point; neither Mohamad's nor Ghaithaa's phones were working, and if we were separated, there would be no way to reach them. On the other hand, Ghaithaa was very sick. I could see it on her face; she wasn't faking.

"OK, do what you want, but if the buses arrive, I won't wait for you." Amer was seething.

"Who told you to wait?" Mohamad didn't care. He went with Ghaithaa to see the volunteers.

"Why did you talk to him in such a tone?" Haya reproved Amer. "You would do the same if I was sick."

"Can we please not talk about it?" Amer was in a rage. We knew him; letting him rage wasn't the best solution, but arguing with him was the last thing we wanted to do. "I should stay in Germany," he said, catching our attention. "Why would I go to Sweden? All the people we know have stayed in Germany."

Apparently, he wasn't joking when he'd asked us if we wanted to stay in Germany.

How long has he been thinking about it? I wondered. *Is this the reason why he is angry with Mohamad?*

"Are you talking for real?" said Othman in a surprised tone.

"Yes, and I swear I would have given my fingerprints here if your parents wouldn't be worried about me leaving you. I would have gone with Laith, but no. I have to stick with you."

Thankfully, he stopped talking, but he left many question marks above my head. I had no idea what had happened to him all of a sudden. If he wanted to stay in Germany, we could discuss it with a conversation, not an argument. *A fight between the brothers, why not? That's just what we need.*

I became exasperated, but I knew that it was better to keep my mouth shut and wait desperately for the bus to end this misery. I was praying that Mohamad would come back before the bus arrived.

We waited in obnoxious, poisoned silence. The longer we waited, the more harm it did to our brains. Othman gestured for me to follow him, and I didn't hesitate to break free. We walked together to a food line, although we had lost our appetite.

"Man, your brothers are dumb. Do they have to fight now?" Othman was as upset as me.

"Forget about it," I said. I didn't want to talk.

There were only a few people in the food line, and there were cheese sandwiches with milk. The second I grabbed a sandwich, I heard Haya saying, "Mohi! Othman! The bus has arrived!"

I put the sandwich back and jogged with Othman outside. Amer was already carrying Abdo. He got on the bus without waiting for anyone.

"Where is Mohamad now?" I growled.

"I don't know. Damn!" Othman ranted.

There was a line of people putting their bags in the baggage and going on the bus through the back door. We had some time to procrastinate. We looked around for Mohamad and Ghaithaa, but it was in vain.

"You go. I will search for him," I told Othman and ran back to the building.

I went back to where we were sitting, and they weren't there. I asked the police where the volunteers were located, I ran there, and they weren't there either. They had disappeared. I didn't know what to do. I went back to Othman, who was explaining the situation to the bus driver.

"There is a fixed time schedule, and we can't delay," the driver said. "And I can't promise that the next bus will go to the same destination you are going to."

The engine started, and everyone was in place. Othman and I went on the bus. I had one last look when I was on the stairs—and I saw Mohamad walking Ghaithaa back slowly to the building.

"Mohamad!" I yelled out loud and waved. "Here, come here!"

I looked at the driver, and he nodded at me. They made it to the bus. I exhaled such a giant sigh that my shoulders dropped to the ground. Mohamad and Ghaithaa sat on seats near the driver, while Amer and Haya sat in the back. Othman was sitting in front of them, and I sat next to him. Before I made myself comfortable, Amer handed Linda to me without saying a word and sat alone on an empty seat away from us.

Linda was half asleep but also upset that her sleeping had been disturbed. It was my duty to bless her. After the bus moved, Othman started snoring with his head leaning against the window, and Linda fell asleep. Almost everyone on the bus was asleep.

I was burning. The windows were all closed, and the heating was on as an extra gift to our drained bodies. I could tell with confidence that open windows and air conditioners are the drivers' worst enemy.

I put Linda in Othman's lap and walked to the driver. The lights were turned off. I nudged and stomped people on the way.

"Tell the driver to turn off the heating. I can't breathe," said one man, grabbing me by the arm.

"Sure," I uttered instead of saying *why don't you tell him yourself?*

The driver's seat was surrounded by duct tape like a spiderweb to prevent people from getting in. It felt like he was sitting in a cage that protected him from wild animals.

"Excuse m—"

Before I finished the word, the driver looked at me from the mirror and moved his hand as a gesture to go back to my territory.

"Excuse me," I repeated firmly. "Can you turn the heating off? It is so hot back there."

"Yeah, I will turn it down. Go back to your seat. You are not supposed to be here." I could tell he just wanted to get rid of me.

"Turn it off," I said as I stared right into his soul. I was fed up with the same issue and the same behaviour every time we got on a bus.

"Here, I lowered it," he said. "Now go back to your seat. You can't be standing while I am driving." His tone changed, or maybe I understood what he meant in the first place—that he was following the safety rules. My head and thoughts were messed up. It was chaotic in there. I didn't know that walking for miles in the rain was much easier than a fight between my brothers.

On my way back, I saw Mohamad covering Ghaithaa with his jacket. She was sick and feeling cold, although the bus was hot. They were both sleeping. I got back to my seat. Linda was almost falling off of Othman's lap, so I took her and could finally sleep after the temperature dropped a little.

At 00:27, the bus stopped at a building. The driver turned on the lights, and people went blind for a couple of seconds. We had arrived in Berlin. We hadn't been told what our destination was, but I had read many signs that said *Berlin* and other German words I didn't understand.

We got off the bus. Othman was feeling dizzy and didn't look well. Maybe he needed more sleep, but he might have been sick as well. We entered the building through the revolving door. It was only our bus that had arrived. Still, the noise of talking people was heard from behind a giant door.

We waited in a reception area in what looked like a waiting room, with a reception desk in front of us. It was another one-storey building with a wide corridor and a vending machine. It looked sort of like a school building.

Half of the people talked to the person at the reception desk, got a yellow paper wristband, and walked through the giant door. It was hard to see what was behind it but easy to hear the noise getting louder each time the door opened and closed.

"So, you are the last. Please come and have a seat!" said the receptionist, who was sitting next to a security guard. "Can I get your passport?" she asked.

"Sorry, but what for?" said Mohamad.

"Just a normal check."

"Are we going to give our fingerprints here? The police at the border said that whoever enters Germany must give their fingerprints. Is that true?"

"Don't listen to what the border police say," said the receptionist. "You are free to decide whether you want to get fingerprinted and stay in Germany or not. Here, I only need to check your passports, and then I am going to give you yellow paper wristbands that you need to show to the security guards when you enter the hall or when you want to eat."

She must have answered the same question hundreds of times, but she still answered in a friendly tone. Finally, some good treatment.

She checked the passports while the security officer wrote our names on the wristbands. We then walked towards the security officer in front of the giant door. We showed our wristbands, and he opened the door for us. Hundreds of people were inside a hall, and the loud noise coming from inside was no longer a mystery.

It was a huge sports hall. The ground was elastic, and for some reason, there were projectors on the ceiling. The place was full of camp beds. A mountain of blankets was in the corner of the building. Surprisingly, there were many empty camp beds. We grabbed some blankets, and as we were getting ready to go to sleep, a security officer near the door said out loud, "The lights will be turned off in five minutes."

It was 01:00, and everyone wanted to get some rest. Othman fell asleep within one minute, while the lights were still on. He was sick for sure. After the lights were shut down, the moonlight made its way gently through the small windows on top of the walls. There was still a remarkable noise of people moving and talking and some crying children, but everything became quiet eventually. Almost everyone fell asleep. I tried, but it wasn't easy.

I looked up at the ceiling while listening to the breaths of people.

We are all alone now. Sleman stayed in Austria, and both Yazan and Laith found their way. We haven't met with Ezz yet—we were supposed to be meeting him from the second day—and I haven't spoken to my brothers for hours. I miss my parents …

Negative thoughts were rushing into my brain, and I had to stop them before I lost my mind. I covered my head with the blanket and meditated on the matte black to force myself to sleep.

15
The Last Station
"And that is why I decided to write a book."

Thursday/22-10-2015/07:25

"Mohi, wake up. Come on, wake up! The breakfast hall closes soon. Come on!" It was Amer.

"Othman, wake up!" he said. "You need to eat and then see if there is medicine for you. Your body temperature is high."

I sat on the narrow camp bed. My leather jacket had drawn a map of the world on my face. People were already awake, and the noise made me wonder how could I sleep in such an environment in the first place.

Amer wasn't lying. The breakfast hall was going to close in half an hour, and after all that had happened, we forgot that we hadn't eaten anything for an entire day. We got up, carried the most important of our stuff, and left the rest on the beds. The building had an underground basement that we hadn't noticed when we arrived. We walked downstairs to what looked like a buffet that served fish paste in addition to sliced bread with jam and butter. Of course, we chose the jam and butter.

Everything went back to normal between us. We never spoke of the argument or apologized. We just understood that everyone was exhausted and fed up with everything. Come to think of it, we needed a small fight to get out our anger.

We ate quickly so that Mohamad, Ghaithaa, and Haya could go back to the stuff we had left without guard. I went with Amer and Othman to a nurse who worked in the building. We had to wait for half an hour because there were two patients ahead of us.

"You are fine," the doctor said to Othman. "It is just a fever due to a sudden change of temperature." She stated the obvious and gave him some pills to lower his temperature.

We got out of the nurse's office and joined Mohamad and the rest. I sat down on the bed and saw someone waving from a distance. I wasn't sure if he was waving at us or somebody else.

"Amer, do you know that guy?" I asked.

"Yes. Finally. This is an Iraqi security guard that I talked to earlier. He might find us a way to get out of here."

Before we could ask him any questions, Amer walked to the security officer and stood there with him for a long period before he came back.

"Who is he?" Mohamad asked the question we all wanted to ask.

"He has a relative who is a taxi driver. He offered to call him to take us to a ferry terminal where we can take a ferry directly to Sweden without going through Denmark," Amer explained. "He also told me that people who arrive in Berlin are left on their own. It is up to us to decide whether we want to stay in Germany or continue to other countries. The government is not responsible for us anymore. Some people have been here for three days or more, he says. So what should I tell him?"

"How much?" asked Mohamad. "Don't tell me 1,200 euros like in Hungary."

"No. I asked him about the price. It is his relative who decides, but it will cost like a normal taxi."

"But Amer, we have only 300 euros or something left. What about the ferry tickets?" I tried to calculate the price, and I was sure it wouldn't be enough.

"We have more," said Amer, making me more confused. "When we were in Athens, Haya's sister knew that we were going to Sweden. Haya didn't tell anyone because she didn't want her family to worry, but her sister kept on calling, and Haya's phone wasn't working, so she called me and I told her. She was so shocked and sad, she wanted to help us, so she sent 400 euros that I picked up from Western Union in Athens. I didn't tell anyone because I didn't want to use the money and wanted to give it back to Haya's sister, but now I think we have to."

I didn't understand what Amer was planning at first, since he knew how much we had, but after what he said, it made sense.

"This is the only solution," said Haya. "Even if we decided to go to Denmark, who knows, Denmark might close its borders or it might cost us more. At least going from Germany to Sweden directly is guaranteed."

We discussed our options and looked up the ferry ticket price, which was around 20 euros. We found out that going to Sweden by ferry was expensive but the safest way. Amer went to the security guard and agreed to the offer.

He came back then and said, "I talked to him. He said his relative will be here in about half an hour, but we have to go outside without anybody noticing, especially the security guards. I will go out first, then you can follow me."

We got ready and followed Amer one by one. We acted normally, as though we were going out to get some fresh air. I was pretty sure some security guards saw us, but according to what we were told, people were on their own, so it was OK for us to go out and back in the building. We searched for the Iraqi security guard in the rain but didn't see him.

"Guys," he whispered from inside the building. "No one can see us together. I'll meet you at the back door. Go there!"

We did as he ordered and walked around the building. There we saw him waiting for us. We waited for five minutes before his relative arrived, and it was more than enough to make us wet from head to toe. The car was grey and could seat eight passengers.

"Hello!" said the driver.

"Hi!" the security guard replied. "These are the people I told you about. They need to go to the ferry terminal. How much will that be?" asked the security guard.

"They are many. I will ask for 75 euros for each. The toddlers can ride for free. Is that OK?"

"I don't know," hesitated Amer after realizing it would cost 450 euros. The driver then suggested 70 euros each. "OK, I guess," said Amer.

We saved 30 euros, but I was sure the driver profited more than he expected. The car had two folding rear seats in the back where Othman and I sat with all our bags. Haya carried Abdo and sat beside Ghaithaa and Mohamad in the middle seats, while Amer sat next to the driver holding Linda.

The car wasn't the only thing that was grey. The sky and the streets were but shades of grey, which made the vibrant orange leaves of the old street trees on both sides of the car stand out shining. People in the streets were used to the daily rain, and it didn't hinder them from doing whatever they wanted. Some were riding bicycles. A young couple was enjoying a walk in the rain while a group of friends was taking a selfie.

"What is the name of the ferry terminal we are going to?" Amer asked the driver.

"It is called *Rostock*," answered the driver. Amer typed the name into Google.

"How much time does it take to reach it?" asked Othman.

"About three and a half hours. You can sleep a little if you want," said the driver.

As much as I wanted to look more through the falling raindrops on the window, hearing that we had more than three hours to reach the terminal made me sleepy. I was surrounded by bags, which I looked at as pillows. I grabbed one and lay my head on it.

I woke up with a pain in my neck. It was tight in the

Othman and me sleeping in the back of the car

back of the car, and my knees were trapped between the front seat and my seat. I had to sleep in a tightly curled foetal position.

The driver stopped at a rest area to get fuel. I looked out the window, and there was nothing to see. We were on the highway, and I felt regret that I hadn't saved my sleep for the highway where there was nothing to see. Slowly, the sea was appearing. Two hours later, we arrived at the ferry terminal.

"The reception where you can buy the ticket is right there," said the driver, pointing. "Have a safe journey!"

We walked into the reception area, ready to lose more money. Two receptionists welcomed us.

"Hello!" asked Othman. "When is the first ferry leaving?"

"I am afraid there aren't any trips soon!" said the receptionist.

"Oh! When is the next trip?" Othman asked.

"The next trip is at 22:30."

Eleven hours of waiting—660 minutes. It would be tough. But the important question was, where were we going to stay?

"I understand that this is a lot to ask for, but can we wait here? As you can see, we have just arrived, and we have no place to go," said Amer.

No way she will agree, I thought.

"Hmm, yeah, I think you can stay," she said. "I will take care of it, so don't worry. But are you going to buy tickets for the next trip?"

It might have been the first time I was happy to be proven wrong.

"Yes, sure," said Amer. "Six tickets for adults and two for kids. How much?"

"That will be 20 euros for adults. Toddlers under 5 years need no tickets."

She checked our passports and returned them with the tickets. It was time for the hardest part: waiting.

The reception office wasn't too big. It had some chairs and a number puzzle mat for kids with some toys which Abdo and Linda played with. Thank God there was a huge television screen to entertain us for the next eleven hours. I sat for half an hour before I decided to explore the reception area in the spare time I had.

I found a corkboard that many papers were pinned to. There were instructions and information about the ferries in both German and English that I didn't bother to read, although I could have read them hundreds of times.

Colourful random drawings by kids filled the board, but what caught my attention the most was the Arabic handwriting of what looked like refugees who had been here before.

"After a long journey, we reached Germany," read one. "There is one station left. Sweden, we are coming!"

"Without doubts, these days are and will always be the most difficult days of my life," read another. "I hope the future holds brighter days."

Another read simply, "Ammar passed from here."

One guy wrote a longer message: "I can never forget these days and what I have gone through. I still remember the night where I laid on my back on the Turkish island and enjoyed the view of a million stars. I can't forget the toughest time we had on the rubber boat and the long walks in the rain. And that is why I decided to write a book, a book about the suffering that we, the Syrian people, are facing, and I am going to name it *The Rain Journey*."

This is a really good idea, I thought. *I will definitely read it once it is published.* Little did I know.

After I counted how many holes there were in the reception chair, I got triggered by that one faulty lamp on the ceiling and noticed that my nose was always in my field of vision and my brain ignored it the whole time. We still had eight hours of pure boredom.

"Are you hungry?" asked Amer.

"Not really. I don't feel like eating anything," answered Haya on behalf of all of us.

"Me neither, but sooner or later, we will feel hungry. Mohi, let's look around for a supermarket near here."

"Wait, I will ask the receptionist," I suggested.

She told us that there was a small market around the port.

The cold wind mixed with water drops hit us in the face as we took our first step outside the office. The market was five minutes away. We weren't sure what to buy. Most of the meat was pork and the beef, and the chicken meat wasn't halal, which minimized our options to the very thing we had been eating throughout the journey: fish. We bought three cans of sardines and a loaf of bread.

"Amer! Look!" I pointed. "Isn't this the black liquorice candy Ezz's father used to bring to us from Germany?"

"Yes, it is," Amer agreed. "May Allah have mercy on him. Our dream as kids was to travel to Germany with him. If only he could see where we are now."

My uncle, Ezz's father, who I was named after, used to export cars from Germany and Syria. He spent most of his life in Germany, and we got excited every time he came back with a brand-new Mercedes or BMW—and, most importantly, the candy and teddy bears he brought to every single one of his nephews and nieces.

As kids, Othman, Ezz, and I were greedy for candies. Ezz always helped us sneak to his father's room so we could steal candies and toys that weren't meant to be ours. Our uncle promised that he would take us with him to Germany one day, but he was gone before he could carry out his promise.

We got out of the market, and I was amazed at how a tiny piece of candy could bring such a sea of memories. If he was alive, getting to Germany wouldn't have been a drag. Yesterday is history and tomorrow is a mystery. No one can predict life.

We returned to the reception office. Amer was about to open the sardine cans before Mohamad stopped him.

"What are you doing?" he said. "Don't open the sardines here. The smell will get us kicked out!"

There was a picnic table outside the office. We went out to eat and get some freezing fresh air. Everyone started eating. I was hungry, but after one bite, my appetite was gone. I almost threw up. *Fish with oil, no thanks*. They finished eating and we scurried back to our cave.

I just wanted to kill some time, and the best way to do it was to sleep, but I couldn't. I had slept on the way to the terminal, and I couldn't put myself to sleep.

After six dead boring hours, two buses filled with refugees arrived at the terminal at 21:30, and people rushed in to buy their tickets to Sweden. It became so crowded that we had to carry our stuff and get out of the office. It was strange. We had been told that once we arrived in Germany, we were on our own, but these two buses that drove here must have been arranged.

"Did we get scammed?" I asked.

"It seems like we did," said Mohamad.

"Maybe the officer told us that people have been in the camp for several days just to make us pay for the taxi," guessed Ghaithaa.

"Excuse me," Amer said to a guy who was on one of the buses. "Did you come here from Berlin?"

"No, we came from Frankfurt," answered the guy before he continued to the office to buy his ticket.

"It can be that the municipalities in Germany have different plans. In Berlin, people are on their own, but in Frankfurt, people get help to move around Germany." Amer came to a conclusion that made us feel a bit better that we didn't get scammed. Maybe.

Before the refugees all bought their tickets, tourists came to buy tickets as well. When it was 22:00, everyone had a ticket, and two minibuses stopped by us. The drivers walked to us and explained that they would drive us to the ferry. I could see the ferry coming toward the terminal, but walking to it would take a long time. That was why there were minibuses.

"Tourists, please follow me," said one bus driver.

They started with the tourists first. Their minibus could take at least eight more people, but when we tried to get on it, we were stopped.

"This minibus is for tourists only," said the driver, blocking the door.

Yes, I was annoyed, but whatever. We took the other minibus. We drove for a couple of minutes before we arrived at the ferry and the minibuses drove back to take the rest.

The ferry was gigantic—a four-floor beast decorated with hundreds of lights and chimneys that looked like horns. Two ferry staff members wearing yellow jackets asked to see our tickets. We climbed the narrow stairs to find another staff member showing us the way to the first floor and blocking the way to the other floors.

There was a restaurant with a bar and many tables and chairs on the first floor, yet staff once again blocked the way. We were all directed to the corner of the hall where there were only four big tables. We were so many we couldn't fit. We sat uncomfortably next to each other.

People were asking the staff for water and to go to the toilets. Instead of treating us like humans, the staff shockingly brought a mobile fence and surrounded the area. It felt like we had been put in a zoo where we were wild animals in cages while tourists walked around and enjoyed the view of crying babies. None of the audience wearing fox-fur overcoats complained. The idea that Abdo and Linda were crying and we couldn't afford the water that was five metres away from us was unbearable.

"Lower your voices, you are making a lot of noise," one staff member insulted us.

That was the breaking point of my patience. At that moment, I was blinded by a five-course serving of rage that tasted bitter.

"What the hell did you just say?" I jeered.

Amer carried Abdo and walked through the mobile fence, knocking it down.

"Hey! You can't go out!" shouted a staff member.

"Hey!" sassed Amer. "What do you want? We are going to book a room. Here is the money that you worship. Can't you see it? We paid the same as those gentle tourists did to get on a ferry. We didn't pay to be put in a barn."

Amer shouted on purpose to make a scene, and he succeeded. The tourists stopped their fancy meal to look over. The distracting noise turned into blank silence in a matter of a second, and everyone was staring at the staff member.

"OK. You can pass, but only you," said the defeated staff member so as not to lose face.

I had lost control and was about to turn into a maniac, but Amer saved the situation smartly. We passed by the staff and climbed the stairs to the second floor to find many refugees there.

"Did they allow you to go to the second floor?" Mohamad asked one guy.

"Yes. Why not?" answered the guy, who didn't understand the purpose of the question.

"The staff didn't allow us to get to the second or third floor."

"I have no idea. The minibuses picked us up after the first group, and when we got here, no one told us where to go."

It wasn't clear if the staff members behaved on their own or were following instructions, but we were happy to get out of that barn.

We sat on the ground like everyone else. We felt that the ferry was finally moving. Abdo and Linda were hungry and crying. It was OK for us to sleep on the floor, but not Abdo and Linda.

"Othman, can you please fill the bottles with water for Abdo and Linda?" Haya asked.

"I will. Why don't we book a room for you to rest in?" suggested Othman.

"No more spending money," said Amer, rejecting the idea. "We don't know what might happen."

"What will happen now? There is nothing to worry about. Tomorrow we will arrive in Sweden." Othman wasn't as careful as Amer when it came to money, but what he said was true, and a room would grant us some very needed comfort. I went with Othman and Haya to the reception to look for a room.

"Hello! Is there an available room?" Haya asked. She had studied English literature and was an English teacher, so there was no need for me and Othman to open our mouths.

"Just give me a second please," answered the receptionist. "Yes, there is an available room with two beds for 83 euros. Would you like to book it?"

A moment of silence and staring passed between Haya and the receptionist. Haya was leaning one hand against the reception desk, and her other hand was in her pocket. The receptionist was smiling awkwardly at Haya, whose eyes were half-closed.

"Haya? She is talking to you?" I told Haya.

"What does she want?" Haya said lethargically in Arabic.

"She is saying that there is room for 83 euros."

"OK, whatever. Just tell her to book it."

"We will take it. Thanks," said Othman.

The receptionist booked the room for us and told us to follow her to the room.

"What is the matter? Your brain is on vacation or what?" laughed Othman.

"I don't know," replied Haya. "I can't even open my eyes, and you want my brain to speak in English?"

We were led to the room we had booked. Haya, Ghaithaa, Abdo, and Linda stayed in the room so they could take a shower and get some rest. Amer, Mohamad, Othman, and I searched for a place to sleep. I saw a guy walking through a door and closing it swiftly without making a noise. We followed him.

When we opened the door, a man I couldn't see hissed, "Come in and close the door without drawing attention!" I got in and closed the door before seeing anything. I saw nothing but black until my eyes adapted to the dark to find out we were in an onboard cinema. The floor was full of people who were about to sleep but couldn't thanks to us.

We walked to the corner and lay down under the red seats so no one could notice us. Of course, the ground wasn't comfortable, but we were happy that Abdo and Linda were sleeping on beds, where they should always sleep.

Friday/23-10-2015/05:13

We woke up early, but this time was like no other. We weren't feeling pain but excitement. We weren't feeling miserable but thrilled. From the deck, we could see Sweden getting closer, slowly but surely.

I moved away from everyone to meditate on the blue monster, and for some reason, it didn't seem as frightening. It was perfectly calm and lovely, carrying us softly to land like a friendly giant. It brought back a flood of memories:

Ezz when he started it all …

Planning secretly behind the guest's back …

The heart-wrenching goodbye to my parents …

Waiting for the bus in the park at night …

Yazan and the view of a million stars …

Laith driving the rubber boat …

Salam Aldeen …

The white card in Greece …

The American volunteer …

The exhausted mother walking to Serbia …

The Serbian taxi driver …

The old man that helped us get the white card in Serbia …

Meeting Sleman and Diyala …

Walking in the forest in Hungary …

Taking the train in Hungary …

Ivona …

Hasan …

Saying goodbye to Sleman and Diyala …

The bridge at the German border …

Saying goodbye to Yazan and Laith's family …

From 10-10-2015 to 23-10-2015:

Thirteen days of my life, not a single minute forgettable …

Thirteen days I thought of my parents before sleeping …

Thirteen days of meeting people and saying goodbye …

Thirteen days I never imagined we would go through …

Thirteen days full of tiredness and memories …

Thirteen days that changed my life completely, and it would never be the same again.

After thirteen days, the ferry slowed down. After thirteen days, we arrived in Sweden—my thirteenth country.

Epilogue

"Well, hello there!"

We met Ezz again in a hotel that had been turned into camp in Malmö. Our meeting didn't last long. He told us that his bus had come before he faded away.

Later, we found out that he got to know a girl named Dania on the journey, and they were married now. The same guest who visited us in Turkey came to visit us the day we arrived in Sweden to close a chapter that started with him.

After we stayed five days in Malmö, we were sent to a village in the south called Hammenhög, where we stayed in a camp for ten months. Then we were sent to Kiruna, a city in the far north of Sweden, to stay for around a year before we finally got our residence permit in 15-06-2017 and moved to Gothenburg to start a new life.

My mother, my father, my sister Alyaa, and my grandmother

Dania, Ezz, me, Abdo, Amer, Haya, Linda,
Mohamad, Ghaithaa and her son, Sam, and Othman

About the Author

My journey started well before 10-10-2015. It started the day I was born.

I was born in Mecca because my father had business in Saudi Arabia. My family went back to Syria when I was still a baby.

When Damascus was unfortunately no longer a safe place, we planned to fly to Egypt for two months until circumstances got better. Those two months turned into a year and a month before we travelled to Turkey, where we lived in Istanbul for two and a half years.

It was then that my brothers and I emigrated to Sweden through Greece, Macedonia, Serbia, Hungary, Croatia, Slovenia, Austria, and Germany.

At first, I thought that the difficulty of living away from home would be being away from home, but it was actually being away from the ones you love. I realized that home is not the place you were born or the place you live; it is the place where you don't feel like a foreigner, the place where you are surrounded by family and friends. I am not sure I have found home yet.

Do I have triskaidekaphobia? Is the number thirteen really unlucky? I don't know, but it changed my life.

My journey didn't finish. This was only thirteen days of it.

And who knows, in the next thirteen days, a new journey might get started.

Say, "It is God who delivers you from it, and from every

disaster. Yet then you associate others with Him."

—Al-An'am, verse 64

Printed in the United States
By Bookmasters